Phonics and Vocabulary Skills Practice & Apply: Grade 4

BY

MYRL SHIREMAN

ISBN 10-digit: 1-58037-131-0
13-digit: 978-1-58037-131-5

Printing No. CD-1353

Mark Twain Media, Inc., Publishers
Distributed by Carson-Dellosa Publishing Company, Inc.

Table of Contents

Table of Contents

Introduction

This book for Grade Four is one of a series that also includes books for Grades Five and Six. Each book is written developmentally, so there is no effort to cover all phonics skills in this Grade Four book. Activities are selected based on the utility the skill will have at the fourth-grade level. For students to become proficient using phonics, maximum practice is required on each emphasized skill.

The phonics and vocabulary exercises in this book are based on several premises: that learning is maximized when the skills taught give consideration to the student's speaking and listening vocabulary, that the basic sight words the student will need to successfully complete the phonics skills activity must be identified and taught, that having the student apply the phonics skills in meaningful context is critical to mastery of the skill, and that a valuable aid to mastery is to have the student write sentences using the phonics skills emphasized.

Many of the phonics skills exercises in this book are repetitious. Activities are purposefully written in this format to ensure mastery learning. Many of the students who are experiencing difficulty in applying phonics skills have not had the opportunity to learn the skills to a mastery level. Phonics is only one of the word-attack skills students should be taught in order to master reading and writing successfully.

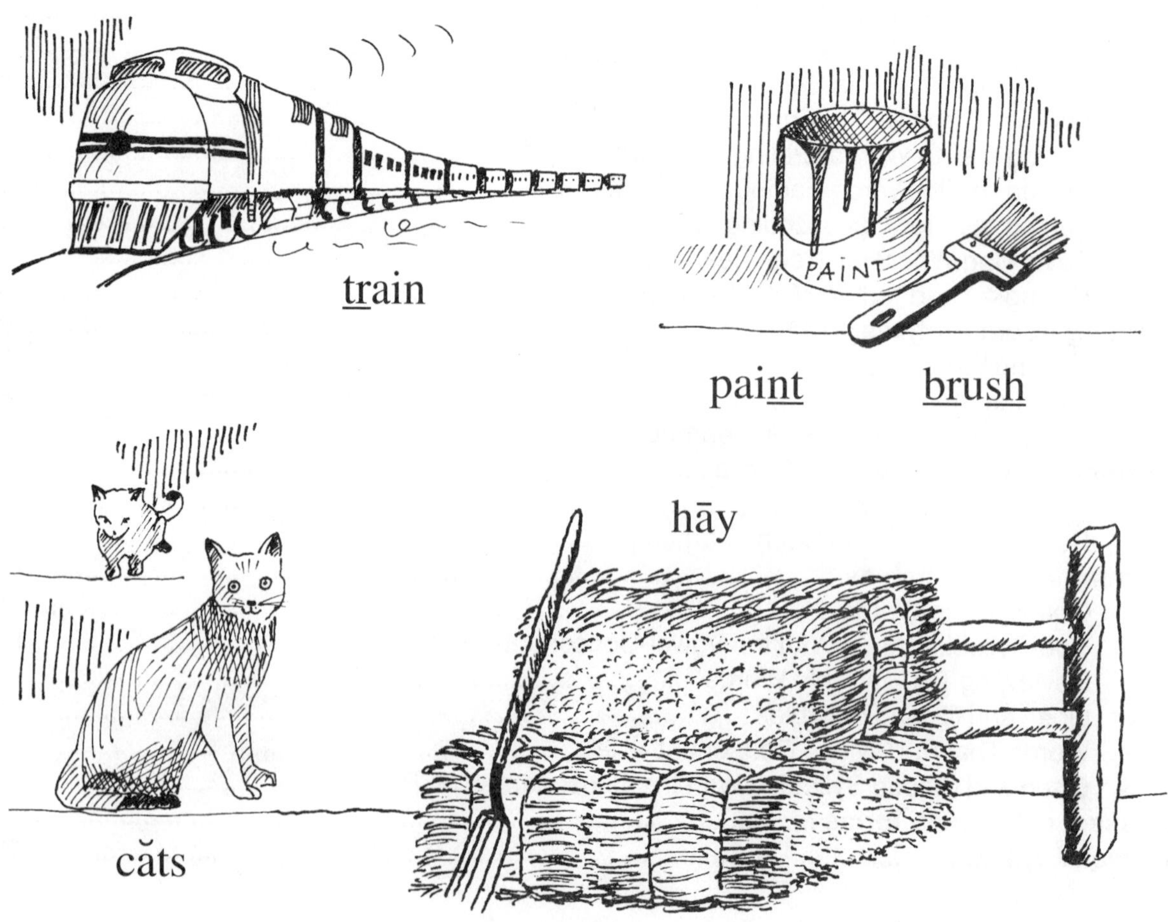

Name: ______________________ Date: ______________

Learning About Consonants: *Making Words With Consonants in the Ending Position*

Make a new word by placing the consonant on the blank at the end of each word. Write the word you have made on the three blanks. Write a sentence using the new word you have made.

p

1. ca___ ___ ___ ___

   Sentence: ______________________

p

2. sa___ ___ ___ ___

   Sentence: ______________________

r

3. ca___ ___ ___ ___

   Sentence: ______________________

n

4. ru___ ___ ___ ___

   Sentence: ______________________

t

5. be___ ___ ___ ___

   Sentence: ______________________

s

6. ga___ ___ ___ ___

   Sentence: ______________________

g

7. fo___ ___ ___ ___

   Sentence: ______________________

t

8. si___ ___ ___ ___

   Sentence: ______________________

Name: ______________________________ Date: ____________________

Learning About Consonants: *The Special Sounds of the Consonant "c"*

The consonants "**c**," "**g**," and "**s**" are special consonants. The sound of each of these consonants depends on the letter that follows the "c," "g," or "s" in a word.

The Consonant "c"

1. When the consonant "c" is followed by the letters "a," "o," or "u," the "c" is pronounced as /k/. Example: The "c" in *cat* is pronounced as /k/.

2. When the consonant "c" is followed by the letters "i" or "e," the "c" is pronounced as /s/. Example: The "c" in *city* is pronounced as /s/.

The Hard and Soft Sounds of "c"

The consonant "c" says /k/ in words like *cat.* This is the hard sound of "c." The consonant "c" says /s/ in words like *cent.* This is the soft sound of "c." Pronounce each of the following words and place the letter /s/ or /k/ on the blank in the following sentences to show which sound the consonant "c" is making in that word.

Sight Words to Know: city, the, drank, milk, it, is, cold, I, live, in, has, twenty, corn

1. The cat drank the milk. /__/ cat
2. It is cold. /__/ cold
3. I live in the city. /__/ city
4. He has twenty cents. /__/ cents
5. The horse ate the corn. /__/ corn
6. She can run fast. /__/ can
7. A plant cell is alive. /__/ cell
8. Cut the pizza in half. /__/ cut

Place the letter **k** or **s** on the blank before each of the following words to show how the consonant "c" is sounded.

1. ___ city
2. ___ cider
3. ___ came
4. ___ cinder
5. ___ come
6. ___ cost
7. ___ center
8. ___ cell
9. ___ cake
10. ___ coke
11. ___ cane
12. ___ cut

Name: ________________________________ Date: ____________________

Learning A out Consonants: *The Special Sounds of the Consonan "c"*

Circle the word c vords in each sentence below that begin with the letter "c." Write the word(s) on the bl ;s and place a /k/ or /s/ on the blanks to show the sound of the letter "c" in the word(s).

Sight Words to | ow: saw, I, in, the, cake, has, cane, candy, do, you, drink, that, is, a, her, white

	k/s	word	k/s	word
1. I saw a car i e city.	___	__________	___	__________
2. The cat ate t cake.	___	__________	___	__________
3. He has a car cane.	___	__________	___	__________
4. The soda co ty cents.	___	__________	___	__________
5. Do you drink er?	___	__________	___	__________
6. That is a cute le.	___	__________	___	__________
7. Her coat is wl	___	__________	___	__________
8. The target is i e center.	___	__________	___	__________

Complete each of t ollowing sentences using one of the words in the box below. Write the letter /k/ or /s/ c e blank to show the pronunciation of the consonant "c" in the word on the blank.

Sights Words to K v: I, think, they, with, me, she, will, how, much, does, did, you, your

	k/s
1. I think I ________ ____ win the race.	___
2. They ________ __ with me yesterday.	___
3. She will ________ ____ tomorrow.	___
4. How much doe cape ____________?	___
5. Did you ________ ____ your finger?	___

came
cost
cut
come
can

Name: ______________________ Date: ______________

Learning About Consonants: *The Special Sounds of the Consonant "g"*

The consonant "g" has a hard sound and a soft sound. The sound of "g" is **hard** in the word *go.* The sound of "g" is **soft** in the word *gym.*

Each of the following words has the consonant "g." Write the letter "h" or "s" on the blank beside each word to indicate if the consonant "g" has a hard or soft sound.

1. ___ go	2. ___ gym	3. ___ gas	4. ___ gum
5. ___ giant	6. ___ gentle	7. ___ germ	8. ___ game
9. ___ glad	10. ___ gave	11. ___ gem	12. ___ got
13. ___ guy	14. ___ good	15. ___ gel	

Complete each of the sentences below using a word from the box. Each word is used only once. Mark the sound of "g" as hard or soft.

Sights Words to Know: I, the, some, fudge, will, horse, be, played, in, is, rode, she, was, to, get

guy	**giant**	**glad**	**gym**	**gum**
gem	**game**	**gave**	**good**	**gentle**

	First Blank	Second Blank
1. I ________ the ________ some fudge.	_ hard _ soft	_ hard _ soft
2. The ________ will be played in the ________.	_ hard _ soft	_ hard _ soft
3. The chewing ________ has a ________ flavor.	_ hard _ soft	_ hard _ soft
4. The huge ________ rode a ________ horse.	_ hard _ soft	_ hard _ soft
5. She was ________ to get the________ necklace.	_ hard _ soft	_ hard _ soft

Name: ______________________ Date: ______________

Learning About Consonants: *The Special Sounds of the Consonant "s"*

In the following words, the letter "s" has either the soft sound of /s/ or the hard sound of /z/. Place an /s/ or /z/ on the blank before each word to indicate if the sound is /s/ or /z/.

1. ____ sit	2. ____ his	3. ____ side	4. ____ so
5. ____ rose	6. ____ us	7. ____ send	8. ____ sun
9. ____ sad	10. ____ see	11. ____ said	12. ____ gust
13. ____ gas	14. ____ busy	15. ____ rise	

Complete each sentence below by using the words in the box. On the blank, indicate if the sound of "s" is /s/ or /z/.

Sight Words to Know: I, will, a, he, would, be, home, letter, of, fudge, soon, flower, very, she, when, sky, clear, for, many, miles, has, long

nose	**rose**	**soap**	**send**	**noise**
see	**sand**	**his**	**said**	**sad**

1. I will ____________ a letter. ___ /s/ ___ /z/
2. He ____________ he would be home soon. ___ /s/ ___ /z/
3. The box of fudge is ____________. ___ /s/ ___ /z/
4. The ____________ is a flower. ___ /s/ ___ /z/
5. She looks very ____________. ___ /s/ ___ /z/
6. When the sky is clear, I can ____________ for many miles. ___ /s/ ___ /z/
7. The animal has a long ____________. ___ /s/ ___ /z/
8. Wash your hands with ____________. ___ /s/ ___ /z/
9. The ____________ on the beach is warm. ___ /s/ ___ /z/
10. Did you hear that ____________? ___ /s/ ___ /z/

Name: ______________________ Date: ______________

Learning About Consonants: *Reviewing the Sounds of "c," "g," and "s"*

Pronounce each of the following words. Place a check mark on the blank to show the sound the consonant in bold makes. Write a sentence using the word.

1. **c**ut ___ /k/ ___ /s/

   Sentence: ______________________

2. **g**ym ___ hard ___ soft

   Sentence: ______________________

3. **c**ome ___ /k/ ___ /s/

   Sentence: ______________________

4. **c**ent ___ /k/ ___ /s/

   Sentence: ______________________

5. **g**one ___ hard ___ soft

   Sentence: ______________________

6. hi**s** ___ /s/ ___ /z/

   Sentence: ______________________

7. **s**ad ___ /s/ ___ /z/

   Sentence: ______________________

8. **c**all ___ /k/ ___ /s/

   Sentence: ______________________

9. ro**s**e ___ /s/ ___ /z/

   Sentence: ______________________

10. **g**em ___ hard ___ soft

    Sentence: ______________________

Name: ______________________________ Date: ____________________

Learning About Consonants: *Reviewing "c" and "g"*

Complete the blanks in each of the following sentences using the letters "c" or "g." Place check marks on the blanks after each question to indicate whether the sound of "c" is /k/ or /s/ and if the sound of "g" is hard or soft.

1. The (a) ___ake you sent is (b) ___ood.

   (a) ___ /k/ ___ /s/ (b) ___ hard ___ soft

2. A (a) ___entle (b) ___amel stood by the (c) ___ate.

   (a) ___ hard ___ soft (b) ___ /k/ ___ /s/ (c) ___ hard ___ soft

3. The (a) ___oach (b) ___ame to the (c) ___ym.

   (a) ___ /k/ ___ /s/ (b) ___ /k/ ___ /s/ (c) ___ hard ___ soft

4. She had a bowl of (a) ___ereal and some (b) ___rapes to eat.

   (a) ___ /k/ ___ /s/ (b) ___ hard ___ soft

5. I (a) ___ot a (b) ___ood (c) ___rade in (d) ___eography.

   (a) ___ hard ___ soft (b) ___ hard ___ soft

   (c) ___ hard ___ soft (d) ___ hard ___ soft

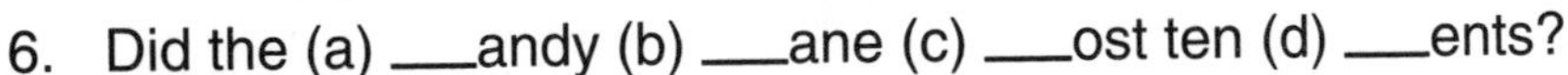

6. Did the (a) ___andy (b) ___ane (c) ___ost ten (d) ___ents?

   (a) ___ /k/ ___ /s/ (b) ___ /k/ ___ /s/

   (c) ___ /k/ ___ /s/ (d) ___ /k/ ___ /s/

7. That (a) ___entle (b) ___iant is a (c) ___ood (d) ___uy.

   (a) ___ hard ___ soft (b) ___ hard ___ soft

   (c) ___ hard ___ soft (d) ___ hard ___ soft

8. I plan to (a) ___ome to the (b) ___ity to play (c) ___olf.

   (a) ___ /k/ ___ /s/ (b) ___ /k/ ___ /s/ (c) ___ hard ___ soft

Name: ______________________ Date: ______________

Learning About Consonants: *Reviewing "c" and "s"*

In each of the following sentences, there are words with the letter "c" or "s" in bold. Place a check mark on the blank to tell the sound the letter "c" or "s" makes in each word.

1. The **c**ity can be a **s**afe place.

   city ___ /k/ ___ /s/ safe ___ /s/ ___ /z/

2. I will **s**end a ro**s**e to each of the boy**s**.

   send ___ /s/ ___ /z/ rose ___ /s/ ___ /z/ boys ___ /s/ ___ /z/

3. This i**s** hi**s** **s**ack.

   is ___ /s/ ___ /z/ his ___ /s/ ___ /z/ sack ___ /s/ ___ /z/

4. Will you plea**s**e give the girl**s** some chee**s**e?

   please ___ /s/ ___ /z/ girls ___ /s/ ___ /z/ cheese ___ /s/ ___ /z/

5. They **s**ing and **s**ail in the **s**un.

   sing ___ /s/ ___ /z/ sail ___ /s/ ___ /z/ sun ___ /s/ ___ /z/

6. Put **s**ome **s**alt in the **s**oup and pass the **c**ookies.

   some ___ /s/ ___ /z/ salt ___ /s/ ___ /z/ soup ___ /s/ ___ /z/

   cookies ___ /k/ ___ /s/

7. **C**an you **s**ee the sun ri**s**e over the tree**s**?

   can ___ /k/ ___ /s/ see ___ /s/ ___ /z/ rise ___ /s/ ___ /z/

   trees ___ /s/ ___ /z/

8. **C**lean the **c**inders from the firepla**c**e before you **s**et out the trash.

   clean ___ /k/ ___ /s/ cinders ___ /k/ ___ /s/

   fireplace ___ /k/ ___ /s/ set ___ /s/ ___ /z/

9. **C**ount the frog**s** in the **c**enter of the pond.

   count ___ /k/ ___ /s/ frogs ___ /s/ ___ /z/

   center ___ /k/ ___ /s/

Name: ______________________________ Date: ____________________

Learning About Vowels: *Making Words With the Short Vowel Sound*

Each of the vowels "a," "e," "i," "o," and "u" makes the short vowel sound. The short sound is marked with a breve (˘).

Place the vowel listed on the blank in each word below. Then write the word you have made again on the three blanks and place the breve symbol (˘) over the vowel to show the short sound. Write a sentence using the new word.

a

1. s__t ___ ___ ___

   Sentence: ________________________________

i

2. s__t ___ ___ ___

   Sentence: ________________________________

e

3. s__t ___ ___ ___

   Sentence: ________________________________

u

4. b__t ___ ___ ___

   Sentence: ________________________________

a

5. b__t ___ ___ ___

   Sentence: ________________________________

i

6. b__t ___ ___ ___

   Sentence: ________________________________

o

7. g__t ___ ___ ___

   Sentence: ________________________________

Name: ______________________________ Date: ______________

Learning About Vowels: *Making Words With the Short Vowel Sound*

Place the vowel listed on the blank in each word below. Then write the word you have made again on the three blanks and place the breve symbol (˘) over the vowel to show the short sound. Write a sentence using the new word.

a

1. m___t ___ ___ ___

   Sentence: ______________________________

e

2. m___t ___ ___ ___

   Sentence: ______________________________

u

3. r___t ___ ___ ___

   Sentence: ______________________________

o

4. r___t ___ ___ ___

   Sentence: ______________________________

i

5. t___n ___ ___ ___

   Sentence: ______________________________

o

6. t___n ___ ___ ___

   Sentence: ______________________________

a

7. t___n ___ ___ ___

   Sentence: ______________________________

u

8. f___n ___ ___ ___

   Sentence: ______________________________

Name: ______________________________ Date: ____________________

Learning About Vowels: *Making Words With the Short Vowel Sound*

Place the vowel listed on the blank in each word below. Then write the word you have made again on the three blanks and place the breve symbol (˘) over the vowel to show the short sound. Write a sentence using the new word.

a

1. f__n __ __ __

   Sentence: ______________________________

i

2. f__n __ __ __

   Sentence: ______________________________

u

3. p__n __ __ __

   Sentence: ______________________________

a

4. p__n __ __ __

   Sentence: ______________________________

i

5. p__n __ __ __

   Sentence: ______________________________

e

6. d__n __ __ __

   Sentence: ______________________________

o

7. n__t __ __ __

   Sentence: ______________________________

u

8. n__t __ __ __

   Sentence: ______________________________

Name: ______________________________ Date: ____________________

Learning About Vowels: *Learning About the Silent "e"*

Some words follow the pattern "long vowel-consonant-silent e." In these words the final "e" is silent. For example, *like* is pronounced with a long "i" and silent "e."

Each of the following words has a short vowel sound. Place the letter "e" on the blank to make a word with a long vowel and a silent "e." Place the macron symbol (¯) over the long vowel and draw a slash through the silent "e." Use each new word in a sentence.

Example: not becomes nōte *I wrote a note.*

1. bit becomes bit__

   Sentence: ______________________________

2. rat becomes rat__

   Sentence: ______________________________

3. fat becomes fat__

   Sentence: ______________________________

4. rod becomes rod__

   Sentence: ______________________________

5. cut becomes cut__

   Sentence: ______________________________

6. pin becomes pin__

   Sentence: ______________________________

7. pan becomes pan__

   Sentence: ______________________________

8. man becomes man__

   Sentence: ______________________________

Name: ______________________ Date: ______________

Learning About Vowels: *Learning About the Silent "e"*

Each of the words below has a long vowel sound with a silent "e." Rewrite each word and place a macron symbol (¯) over the vowel that is long and draw a slash (/) through the silent "e." Use a dictionary to determine the meaning of each word. Pronounce each word and write a sentence using each word.

1. **mile** m ī l e̸
   Meaning: ______________________
   Sentence: ______________________
2. **rime** __ __ __ __
   Meaning: ______________________
   Sentence: ______________________
3. **rule** __ __ __ __
   Meaning: ______________________
   Sentence: ______________________
4. **home** __ __ __ __
   Meaning: ______________________
   Sentence: ______________________
5. **mule** __ __ __ __
   Meaning: ______________________
   Sentence: ______________________
6. **poke** __ __ __ __
   Meaning: ______________________
   Sentence: ______________________
7. **fate** __ __ __ __
   Meaning: ______________________
   Sentence: ______________________
8. **wave** __ __ __ __
   Meaning: ______________________
   Sentence: ______________________

Name: ______________________ Date: ______________

Learning About Vowels: *Learning About the Silent "e"*

Each of the words below has a long vowel sound with a silent "e." Rewrite each word and place a macron symbol (¯) over the vowel that is long and draw a slash (/) through the silent "e." Use a dictionary to determine the meaning of each word. Pronounce each word and write a sentence using each word.

1. **late** ___ ___ ___ ___
   Meaning: ______________________
   Sentence: ______________________
2. **safe** ___ ___ ___ ___
   Meaning: ______________________
   Sentence: ______________________
3. **role** ___ ___ ___ ___
   Meaning: ______________________
   Sentence: ______________________
4. **bile** ___ ___ ___ ___
   Meaning: ______________________
   Sentence: ______________________
5. **bone** ___ ___ ___ ___
   Meaning: ______________________
   Sentence: ______________________
6. **lute** ___ ___ ___ ___
   Meaning: ______________________
   Sentence: ______________________
7. **mete** ___ ___ ___ ___
   Meaning: ______________________
   Sentence: ______________________
8. **pile** ___ ___ ___ ___
   Meaning: ______________________
   Sentence: ______________________

Name: ______________________ Date: ______________

Learning About Vowels: *Learning About the Silent "e"*

Each of the words below has a long vowel sound with a silent "e." Rewrite each word and place a macron symbol (¯) over the vowel that is long and draw a slash (/) through the silent "e." Use a dictionary to determine the meaning of each word. Pronounce each word and write a sentence using each word.

1. **wade** __ __ __ __

   Meaning: ______________________

   Sentence: ______________________

2. **save** __ __ __ __

   Meaning: ______________________

   Sentence: ______________________

3. **rile** __ __ __ __

   Meaning: ______________________

   Sentence: ______________________

4. **file** __ __ __ __

   Meaning: ______________________

   Sentence: ______________________

5. **yule** __ __ __ __

   Meaning: ______________________

   Sentence: ______________________

6. **cute** __ __ __ __

   Meaning: ______________________

   Sentence: ______________________

7. **cone** __ __ __ __

   Meaning: ______________________

   Sentence: ______________________

8. **rope** __ __ __ __

   Meaning: ______________________

   Sentence: ______________________

Name: ______________________________ Date: ____________________

Learning About Vowels: *Learning About the Silent "e"*

Sight Words to Know:

	I	the	saw	rabbit	in
caused	waves	on	when	into	sky
see	many	can	be	a	small
and	dock	with	led	to	house
hill	all	day	fast	would	

Each of the following sentences contains a word with a long vowel sound and a silent "e" at the end. Find the word and write it on the blank following the sentence. Mark the word using the macron (¯) and slash (/) to show the correct pronunciation. On the blank below the sentence, tell what the word means in the sentence.

1. In the vale, I saw a small rabbit. ______________

   ____

2. The gale caused the ripples on the pond. ______________

   ____

3. When I gaze into the clear night sky, I see many stars. ______________

   ____

4. Rats can be trained to run a maze. ______________

   ____

5. The vane turned in the wind and pointed north. ______________

   ____

6. The bale of cotton was on the dock. ______________

   ____

7. He walked with a cane. ______________

   ____

8. The lane led to a house on a hill. ______________

   ____

9. We walked all day at a fast pace. ______________

   ____

Name: ______________________________ Date: ____________________

Learning About Vowels: *Learning About the Silent "e" (continued)*

10. She is hale and hearty. ____________

____

11. A huge animal was in the zoo. ____________

____

12. The note said that the school party would be Friday. ____________

____

Sight Words to Know: I rode the do you feel they new house plan to he broke is

Complete each of the following sentences using the words in the box below. Write each word on the dashed lines and mark each word to show the correct pronunciation.

wade	home	rope	yule	mile
take	safe	lake	rule	mule

1. I rode the __________ to the barn. __ __ __ __
2. Do you feel __________? __ __ __ __
3. Come here and skip __________ with me. __ __ __ __
4. They plan to __________ in the water. __ __ __ __
5. He broke the __________. __ __ __ __
6. Christmas is the __________ season. __ __ __ __
7. He ran a __________ today. __ __ __ __
8. Are you going __________ now? __ __ __ __
9. Would you __________ our picture? __ __ __ __
10. Are there any fish in that __________? __ __ __ __

Name: ______________________ Date: ______________

Learning About Vowels: *Learning About the Silent "e"*

Use the following blends to make new words. **Blends** are two or more consonants that are sounded together. The sound of each consonant can clearly be heard. Write a blend on the blanks before each word part, and then write the new word on the dashed line using the macron (¯) to show the long vowel sound and the slash (/) to show the silent "e" for each word. Write the new word in a sentence.

bl gr pl tr sh sl cr pr st

1. ___ ___ade ___ ___ ___ ___ ___

   Sentence: ______________________

2. ___ ___ate ___ ___ ___ ___ ___

   Sentence: ______________________

3. ___ ___ake ___ ___ ___ ___ ___

   Sentence: ______________________

4. ___ ___ime ___ ___ ___ ___ ___

   Sentence: ______________________

5. ___ ___ude ___ ___ ___ ___ ___

   Sentence: ______________________

6. ___ ___ape ___ ___ ___ ___ ___

   Sentence: ______________________

7. ___ ___ame ___ ___ ___ ___ ___

   Sentence: ______________________

8. ___ ___une ___ ___ ___ ___ ___

   Sentence: ______________________

9. ___ ___ope ___ ___ ___ ___ ___

   Sentence: ______________________

10. ___ ___ave ___ ___ ___ ___ ___

    Sentence: ______________________

Name: ______________________________ Date: ____________________

Learning About Vowels: *Learning About the Silent "e"*

Replace the blends in the words listed under the **Word** column with one of the blends below to make a new word. Use the new word in a sentence. Show the correct markings for long vowel sounds and silent letters.

br gr scr tr bl sl pr st

Word	New Word	New Word With Markings For Vowel Sound and Silent Letters
1. crate	__ __ate	____________
Sentence: ____________		
2. grope	__ __ope	____________
Sentence: ____________		
3. shave	__ __ave	____________
Sentence: ____________		
4. crime	__ __ime	____________
Sentence: ____________		
5. grave	__ __ave	____________
Sentence: ____________		
6. shame	__ __ame	____________
Sentence: ____________		
7. grime	__ __ime	____________
Sentence: ____________		
8. crude	__ __ude	____________
Sentence: ____________		
9. grape	__ __ __ape	____________
Sentence: ____________		
10. grace	__ __ace	____________
Sentence: ____________		

Name: ______________________ Date: ______________

Learning About Vowels: *Learning About the Silent "e"*

Each of the following words has a long "a," "i," or "o" sound and a silent "e." Write the definition of the word. Pronounce the word and use the word in a sentence.

1. **glaze** Definition: ______________________
   Sentence: ______________________
2. **prime** Definition: ______________________
   Sentence: ______________________
3. **vile** Definition: ______________________
   Sentence: ______________________
4. **smote** Definition: ______________________
   Sentence: ______________________
5. **ruse** Definition: ______________________
   Sentence: ______________________
6. **fume** Definition: ______________________
   Sentence: ______________________
7. **brine** Definition: ______________________
   Sentence: ______________________
8. **knave** Definition: ______________________
   Sentence: ______________________
9. **strode** Definition: ______________________
   Sentence: ______________________
10. **bale** Definition: ______________________
    Sentence: ______________________

Name: ______________________________ Date: ________________

Learning About Vowels: *Reviewing What Has Been Learned*

Complete each of the following blanks.

1. Change the **s** in **sat** to **b** to make the word (a) ________. Make a sentence using the new word. (b) ______________________________
2. Change the **t** in **sat** to **d** to make the word (a) ________. Make a sentence using the new word. (b) ______________________________
3. Change the **c** in **can** to **f** to make the word (a) ________. Make a sentence using the new word. (b) ______________________________
4. Change the **n** in **can** to **b** to make the word (a) ________. Make a sentence using the new word. (b) ______________________________
5. Add the letter **e** to **can** to make the word (a) ________. The vowel sound for **a** in **cane** is the (b) ________ sound and the vowel letter **e** is (c) ________. Make a sentence using the new word. (d) ______________________________

____

Change the blend to make a new word. Use the new word in a sentence.

1. Change the **br** in **bray** to **spr** to make the word ______________.
   Sentence: ______________________________
2. Change the **pl** in **plate** to **sl** to make the word ______________.
   Sentence: ______________________________
3. Change the **dr** in **drab** to **cr** to make the word ______________.
   Sentence: ______________________________
4. Change the **fl** in **flare** to **gl** to make the word ______________.
   Sentence: ______________________________
5. Change the **sh** in **shame** to **fl** to make the word ______________.
   Sentence: ______________________________

Name: ________________________ Date: ______________

Learning About Vowels: *Reviewing What Has Been Learned*

Each of the following words has a long or short vowel sound. Some words also have a silent vowel. Complete the blanks for each word. The first one has been completed.

	Word	Vowel Sound Letter	Long/Short Sound	Silent Vowel Letter
1.	sat	a	short	____
2.	sale	____	________	____
3.	fate	____	________	____
4.	fat	____	________	____
5.	mat	____	________	____
6.	mate	____	________	____
7.	cone	____	________	____
8.	vote	____	________	____
9.	bit	____	________	____
10.	bite	____	________	____
11.	cub	____	________	____
12.	cube	____	________	____
13.	mete	____	________	____
14.	met	____	________	____
15.	tube	____	________	____
16.	tub	____	________	____
17.	pet	____	________	____
18.	pole	____	________	____
19.	line	____	________	____
20.	lip	____	________	____

Name: ______________________________ Date: ____________________

Learning About Vowels: *Reviewing What Has Been Learned*

Complete each of the following blanks using the words in the box.

Sight Words to Know:

	is	a	small	bear	do
you	want	me	to	for	water
the	cold	he	said	his	an
in	they	put	go	and	will
my	of	happy	boy	dog	lid
wait	make	good	does	fell	down
my	will	up	flag		

1. A __________ is a small bear.
2. Do you want me to __________ for you?
3. The water in the __________ is cold.
4. He said he wanted an ice __________ in his soda.
5. Put the lid on the toothpaste __________.
6. I want to go to the __________ and buy a cape.
7. Will you want a __________ of my fudge?
8. He __________ on the __________ on the floor.
9. The __________ was a happy young boy.
10. The father dog's __________ is the mother of the puppies.
11. They put the ice cream in a __________.
12. We have to wait in __________ for lunch.
13. Does a lizard make a good __________?
14. I fell down and split my __________.
15. Will you raise the flag up the __________?

vote
lip
sat
sale
pet
cube
line
bite
mate
cub
tube
pole
lad
mat
cone
tub

Name: ______________________ Date: ______________

Learning About Consonant Blends: *Blends at the Beginning of Words*

Consonant blends are two or more consonants grouped together. When the blend is pronounced, each consonant is sounded. Consonant blends are found in many words. Blends may be found at the beginning of a word, in the middle, or at the end of a word.

Example: In the words ***black*** and ***brat,*** the consonant blends are "bl" and "br." The sounds of both consonants are heard when the words are pronounced.

Beginning Blends

Consonant blends are found at the beginning of many words. The word ***gray*** has the beginning blend "**gr.**" Notice that the sounds of both letters in the blend are heard.

Place one of the following consonant blends on the blanks to make a word. Then write the new word on the blanks. Pronounce the word slowly to hear the sounds of both letters in the blend. Write the vowel letter in the word on the blank and then write *long* or *short* to identify the vowel sound. Finally, write a sentence using the word you have made.

bl cl fl gl pl sl

	Blend	New Word	Vowel Letter	Vowel Sound (long/short)
1.	___ ___at	___ ___ ___ ___	___	__________
	Sentence: ______________________________			
2.	___ ___im	___ ___ ___ ___	___	__________
	Sentence: ______________________________			
3.	___ ___am	___ ___ ___ ___	___	__________
	Sentence: ______________________________			
4.	___ ___ad	___ ___ ___ ___	___	__________
	Sentence: ______________________________			
5.	___ ___an	___ ___ ___ ___	___	__________
	Sentence: ______________________________			
6.	___ ___ob	___ ___ ___ ___	___	__________
	Sentence: ______________________________			

Name: ______________________________ Date: ________________

Learning About Consonant Blends: *Blends at the Beginning of Words*

Place one of the following consonant blends on the blanks to make a word. Write the new word on the blanks. Then pronounce the word slowly to hear the sounds of both letters in the blend. Write the vowel letter in the word on the blank and then write *long* or *short* to identify the vowel sound. Finally, write a sentence using the word you have made.

br cr dr fr gr pr tr

Blend	New Word	Vowel Letter	Vowel Sound (long/short)
1. ___ ___at	___ ___ ___ ___	___	________
Sentence: ________________			
2. ___ ___im	___ ___ ___ ___	___	________
Sentence: ________________			
3. ___ ___ab	___ ___ ___ ___	___	________
Sentence: ________________			
4. ___ ___og	___ ___ ___ ___	___	________
Sentence: ________________			
5. ___ ___an	___ ___ ___ ___	___	________
Sentence: ________________			
6. ___ ___ag	___ ___ ___ ___	___	________
Sentence: ________________			
7. ___ ___um	___ ___ ___ ___	___	________
Sentence: ________________			
8. ___ ___ip	___ ___ ___ ___	___	________
Sentence: ________________			
9. ___ ___om	___ ___ ___ ___	___	________
Sentence: ________________			
10. ___ ___im	___ ___ ___ ___	___	________
Sentence: ________________			

Name: ______________________ Date: ______________

Learning About Consonant Blends: *Blends at the Beginning of Words*

Place one of the following consonant blends on the blanks to make a word. Write the new word on the blanks. Then pronounce the word slowly to hear the sounds of both letters in the blend. Write the vowel letter in the word on the blank and then write *long* or *short* to identify the vowel sound. Finally, write a sentence using the word you have made.

sk sm sn sp st sw

	Blend	New Word	Vowel Letter	Vowel Sound (long/short)
1.	___ ___im	___ ___ ___ ___	___	__________
	Sentence: ______________________			
2.	___ ___og	___ ___ ___ ___	___	__________
	Sentence: ______________________			
3.	___ ___ip	___ ___ ___ ___	___	__________
	Sentence: ______________________			
4.	___ ___ud	___ ___ ___ ___	___	__________
	Sentence: ______________________			
5.	___ ___em	___ ___ ___ ___	___	__________
	Sentence: ______________________			
6.	___ ___ap	___ ___ ___ ___	___	__________
	Sentence: ______________________			
7.	___ ___it	___ ___ ___ ___	___	__________
	Sentence: ______________________			
8.	___ ___ug	___ ___ ___ ___	___	__________
	Sentence: ______________________			
9.	___ ___ub	___ ___ ___ ___	___	__________
	Sentence: ______________________			
10.	___ ___ot	___ ___ ___ ___	___	__________
	Sentence: ______________________			

Name: ____________________ Date: ______________

Learning About Consonant Blends: *Blends at the Beginning of Words*

Place one of the following consonant blends on the blanks to make a word. Write the new word on the blanks. Then pronounce the word slowly to hear the sounds of both letters in the blend. Write the vowel letter in the word on the blank and then write *long* or *short* to identify the vowel sound. Finally, write a sentence using the word you have made.

scr **spr** **str** **spl**

	Blend	New Word	Vowel Letter	Vowel Sound (long/short)
1.	__ __ __um	__ __ __ __ __	__	________
	Sentence: ________________			
2.	__ __ __int	__ __ __ __ __ __	__	________
	Sentence: ________________			
3.	__ __ __ap	__ __ __ __ __	__	________
	Sentence: ________________			
4.	__ __ __ig	__ __ __ __ __	__	________
	Sentence: ________________			

Write a word using each of the consonant blends below. Be sure to write words that have consonant blends in the beginning position.

1. bl ____________ 2. cl ____________ 3. scr ____________
4. sn ____________ 5. fr ____________ 6. sw ____________
7. tr ____________ 8. st ____________ 9. spl ____________
10. sp ____________ 11. cr ____________ 12. br ____________
13. gl ____________ 14. pr ____________ 15. fl ____________

Name: ______________________________ Date: ____________________

Learning About Consonant Blends: *Words With Ending Consonant Blends*

In many words, two or more letters at the end of the word form a **consonant blend**. These are consonant pairs at the end of words in which the sound of each consonant is sounded when the blend is pronounced.

The words in the box end with one of the consonant blends "ft," "lk," "nt," or "nd." Choose one of the words from the box to complete the blank found in each sentence. On the blank after the sentence, write the letters that make up the ending blend in the word that completes the sentence.

Sight Words to Know:

	threw	began	toward	with	his
the	pretty	got	dress	her	had
lunch	after	and	will	us	to
money	tickets	hair	large	best	been

		Ending Blend	
1.	He threw the ball with his ____________ hand.	_____	**walk**
2.	I have found the bird that fell to the ____________.	_____	**paint**
3.	They have ____________ the money for the tickets.	_____	**left**
4.	The snow felt as ____________ as cotton.	_____	**cents**
5.	I think the ticket will cost fifty ____________.	_____	**sent**
6.	We'll need a ____________ brush.	_____	**soft**
7.	Let's take a ____________ in the park.	_____	**drift**
8.	She got a pretty dress as a ____________ for her birthday.	_____	**blond**
9.	She has ____________ hair.	_____	**aunt**
10.	The sailboat began to ____________ toward the beach.	_____	**pound**
11.	We will not need a ____________ of meat.	_____	**gift**
12.	Our uncle and ____________ will take us to the game.	_____	**ground**

Name: ______________________________ Date: ____________________

Learning About Consonant Blends: *Words With Ending Consonant Blends*

Write a sentence using each word below. Write the **ending consonant blend** found in each word on the blank beside each word.

1. **swift** _____

   Sentence: ____

2. **bunt** _____

   Sentence: ____

3. **blind** _____

   Sentence: ____

4. **silk** _____

   Sentence: ____

5. **lift** _____

   Sentence: ____

6. **point** _____

   Sentence: ____

7. **brand** _____

   Sentence: ____

8. **grand** _____

   Sentence: ____

9. **loft** _____

   Sentence: ____

10. **tent** _____

    Sentence: ____

Name: ______________________________ Date: ____________________

Learning About Consonant Blends: *Other Two-Letter Consonant Blends at the End of Words*

The two-letter consonant blends "ng," "nk," "pt," "st," and "sp" are also often found at the end of words.

Match the word in Column A with the definition in Column B by placing the correct letter from Column B on the line next to each word in Column A. Then write the ending consonant blend on the blank next to the word in Column A.

	Column A	Ending Consonant Blend	Column B
____	1. clang	____	a. water frozen on grass in the morning
____	2. pink	____	b. what a bird lives in
____	3. boast	____	c. the ruler of a land
____	4. grasp	____	d. opposite of east
____	5. frost	____	e. past tense of keep
____	6. feast	____	f. to brag
____	7. blink	____	g. a stinging insect
____	8. wept	____	h. what the eyes do
____	9. nest	____	i. past tense of sleep
____	10. west	____	j. a color
____	11. wasp	____	k. a circular object
____	12. slept	____	l. cried
____	13. ring	____	m. lots of food
____	14. kept	____	n. to hold tight
____	15. king	____	o. the sound a bell makes

Name: ______________________ Date: ____________

Learning About Consonant Blends: *Other Two-Letter Consonant Blends at the End of Words*

Write a sentence using each of the following words. First, circle the ending blend in each word. Then, write the ending blend on the two blanks following the word. Finally, write a sentence using the word.

1. **drink** ___ ___

   Sentence: ______________________

2. **crisp** ___ ___

   Sentence: ______________________

3. **blast** ___ ___

   Sentence: ______________________

4. **thirst** ___ ___

   Sentence: ______________________

5. **bring** ___ ___

   Sentence: ______________________

6. **prank** ___ ___

   Sentence: ______________________

7. **crept** ___ ___

   Sentence: ______________________

8. **except** ___ ___

   Sentence: ______________________

9. **vast** ___ ___

   Sentence: ______________________

10. **fang** ___ ___

    Sentence: ______________________

Name: ____________________ Date: ____________

Learning About Consonant Blends: *Words That End in "dge"*

Many words, such as *fudge*, end with the letters "dge." When a word ends with "dge," the "e" is silent.

Sight Words to Know: the man was think we will play a horse stood on

Each of the following sentences has a word that ends with the letters "dge." Underline the word in each sentence that ends with "dge." Draw a slash (/) through the final "e" to show that the "e" is silent. Mark the vowel sound of the other vowel in the word, using the breve symbol (˘) to show the short vowel sound. Use the dictionary and write the dictionary pronunciation for each of the "dge" words. Then make a new sentence using the word.

Dictionary Pronunciation of "dge" Word

1. The man was eating fudge. ____________

   Sentence: ____________________

2. I think we will play bridge. ____________

   Sentence: ____________________

3. The policeman wore a badge. ____________

   Sentence: ____________________

4. A horse stood on the ridge. ____________

   Sentence: ____________________

5. The judge sat on the bench. ____________

   Sentence: ____________________

6. How many vowels do you see in each of the "dge" words above? ____________
7. When you pronounce each "dge" word, how many vowel sounds do you hear?

   ____

8. When you see "dge" at the end of a word, you expect the "e" to be (silent/sounded).

Name: ______________________ Date: ______________

Learning About Consonant Blends: *Words That End in "dge"*

Find each of the following "dge" words in the dictionary. Write the dictionary pronunciation on the blank and a meaning for each word. Use the word correctly in a sentence.

	Word	Dictionary Pronunciation	Meaning
1.	trudge	________	____________________
	Sentence: ____________________		
2.	grudge	________	____________________
	Sentence: ____________________		
3.	pledge	________	____________________
	Sentence: ____________________		
4.	smudge	________	____________________
	Sentence: ____________________		
5.	ledge	________	____________________
	Sentence: ____________________		

Complete the blanks using one of the blends below to make a word.

dge ft nt nd ng pt sp st

1. lo ___ ___ ___	2. se ___ ___	3. gi ___ ___
4. ba ___ ___ ___	5. sa ___ ___	6. ke ___ ___
7. be ___ ___	8. co ___ ___	9. e ___ ___ ___
10. dri ___ ___	11. te ___ ___	12. sta ___ ___
13. sa ___ ___	14. sle ___ ___	15. cri ___ ___
16. du ___ ___	17. we ___ ___ ___	18. fro ___ ___
19. we ___ ___	20. li ___ ___	

Name: ______________________________ Date: ____________________

Learning About Vowel Pairs: *Learning About the "ai" Vowel Pair*

Sight Words to Know: is, a, will, I, the, we, to, city, for, they, all, day, went, took, careful, thought, would, decided, arm

In each of the following sentences, you will find a word with the letters "ai." When these two letters are together, they make the long sound of the letter "a." Read each sentence. Then write the word with the letters "ai" on the blanks in Column I. Write the letters "ai" on the blanks in Column II. On the blanks in Column III, write the sound that the letters "ai" make.

	Column I (Word)	**Column II (Vowel Pair)**	**Column III (Vowel Sound)**
1. Corn is a grain.	_ _ _ _ _	_ _	_
2. I will sail the boat.	_ _ _ _	_ _	_
3. I thought I would faint.	_ _ _ _ _	_ _	_
4. Father paid for the meal.	_ _ _ _	_ _	_
5. They decided to paint the house white.	_ _ _ _ _	_ _	_
6. The rain fell all day.	_ _ _ _	_ _	_
7. There was a lot of pain in my arm.	_ _ _ _	_ _	_
8. He took careful aim.	_ _ _	_ _	_
9. The hail fell for an hour.	_ _ _ _	_ _	_
10. We rode the train to the city.	_ _ _ _ _	_ _	_

Name: ______________________________ Date: ____________________

Learning About Vowel Pairs: *Learning About the "ai" Vowel Pair*

Place one of the following consonants on each blank to make a word. Write the word on the blanks under Column I. Write the letters that make the long "a" sound on the blanks under Column II. Write a sentence using each word.

h n m p t b f j r s

	Column I (Word)	Column II (Vowel Pair)
1. __ail	__ __ __ __	__ __
2. __ail	__ __ __ __	__ __
3. __ail	__ __ __ __	__ __
4. __ail	__ __ __ __	__ __
5. __ail	__ __ __ __	__ __
6. __ail	__ __ __ __	__ __
7. __ail	__ __ __ __	__ __
8. __ail	__ __ __ __	__ __
9. __ail	__ __ __ __	__ __
10. __ail	__ __ __ __	__ __

1. __ail __ __ __ __ __ __

   Sentence: ______________________________

2. __ail __ __ __ __ __ __

   Sentence: ______________________________

3. __ail __ __ __ __ __ __

   Sentence: ______________________________

4. __ail __ __ __ __ __ __

   Sentence: ______________________________

5. __ail __ __ __ __ __ __

   Sentence: ______________________________

6. __ail __ __ __ __ __ __

   Sentence: ______________________________

7. __ail __ __ __ __ __ __

   Sentence: ______________________________

8. __ail __ __ __ __ __ __

   Sentence: ______________________________

9. __ail __ __ __ __ __ __

   Sentence: ______________________________

10. __ail __ __ __ __ __ __

   Sentence: ______________________________

Name: ______________________________ Date: ____________________

Learning About Vowel Pairs: *Learning About the "ay" Vowel Pair*

In each of the following sentences you will find a word with the letters "ay." When these two letters are together, they make the long sound of the letter "a." Read each sentence. Then write the word with the letters "ay" on the blanks in Column I. Write the letters "ay" on the blanks in Column II. Finally, on the blank under Column III, write long "a" or short "a" to show the sound the "ay" pair makes.

	Column I (Word)	Column II (Vowel Pair)	Column III (long "a"/ short "a")
1. The mule ran away.	_ _ _ _	_ _	________
2. She may not go.	_ _ _	_ _	________
3. Don't stay too late.	_ _ _ _	_ _	________
4. Put the fudge on the tray.	_ _ _ _	_ _	________
5. Use the hose to spray water.	_ _ _ _ _	_ _	________
6. The color is gray.	_ _ _ _	_ _	________
7. They went out to play.	_ _ _ _	_ _	________
8. The relay team won the race.	_ _ _ _ _	_ _	________
9. That dog is a stray.	_ _ _ _ _	_ _	________
10. I saw a boat in the bay.	_ _ _	_ _	________
11. Get out of my way!	_ _ _	_ _	________
12. The wind makes the trees sway.	_ _ _ _	_ _	________
13. The donkey let out a loud bray.	_ _ _ _	_ _	________
14. The man went to slay the dragon.	_ _ _ _	_ _	________
15. That pot is made of clay.	_ _ _ _	_ _	________

Name: ______________________________ Date: __________________

Learning About Vowel Pairs: *Learning About the "ay" Vowel Pair*

Place one of the following consonant blends on the blanks to make a word. Write the word on the blanks in Column I. Then write the letters that make the long "a" sound on the blanks in Column II. Finally, write a sentence using the word.

pl st sl gr tr cl spr str pr spl

	Column I (Word)	Column II (Vowel Pair)
1. ___ ___ay	___ ___ ___ ___	___ ___
Sentence: ______________________________		
2. ___ ___ay	___ ___ ___ ___	___ ___
Sentence: ______________________________		
3. ___ ___ay	___ ___ ___ ___	___ ___
Sentence: ______________________________		
4. ___ ___ay	___ ___ ___ ___	___ ___
Sentence: ______________________________		
5. ___ ___ay	___ ___ ___ ___	___ ___
Sentence: ______________________________		
6. ___ ___ay	___ ___ ___ ___	___ ___
Sentence: ______________________________		
7. ___ ___ ___ay	___ ___ ___ ___ ___	___ ___
Sentence: ______________________________		
8. ___ ___ ___ay	___ ___ ___ ___ ___	___ ___
Sentence: ______________________________		
9. ___ ___ay	___ ___ ___ ___	___ ___
Sentence: ______________________________		
10. ___ ___ ___ay	___ ___ ___ ___ ___	___ ___
Sentence: ______________________________		

Name: ______________________ Date: ______________

Learning About Vowel Pairs: *Reviewing "ai" and "ay" Vowel Pairs*

Read each sentence. Write the words with the letters "ai" that make the long "a" sound on the blanks in Column I. Write the words with the letters "ay" that make the long "a" sound on the blanks in Column II.

	Column I "ai" Word	Column II "ay" Word
1. I will wait for you to play.	________	________
2. Do they aim to stay?	________	________
3. The nail is in the tray.	________	________
4. Use the gray paint.	________	________
5. I may mail the letter.	________	________
6. Do you plan to sail in the bay?	________	________
7. You pay for the bait.	________	________
8. You must wait to use the crayon.	________	________
9. Did he spray water in the pail?	________	________
10. The mail came late today.	________	________

Each of the following words has the letters "ai" or "ay," which make the long "a" sound. Underline the "ai" or "ay" in each word. If the word has "ai," write "ai" on the blank under Column I. If the word has "ay," write "ay" on the blank under Column II. Write the long vowel sound the letters make on the blank under Column III.

Word	Column I "ai"	Column II "ay"	Column III
1. plain	______	______	______
2. gray	______	______	______
3. daily	______	______	______
4. bray	______	______	______
5. nay	______	______	______
6. praise	______	______	______
7. gaily	______	______	______
8. gait	______	______	______
9. stray	______	______	______
10. maize	______	______	______

Name: ______________________________ Date: ________________

Learning About Vowel Pairs: *Reviewing "ai" and "ay" Vowel Pairs*

Use each of the following words in a sentence. If you are not sure of the meaning of a word, find the meaning in the dictionary.

1. fray: ______________________________
2. nay: ______________________________
3. praise: ______________________________
4. gaily: ______________________________
5. flay: ______________________________
6. plain: ______________________________
7. gray: ______________________________
8. daily: ______________________________
9. gait: ______________________________
10. clay: ______________________________
11. maize: ______________________________
12. bray: ______________________________

Name: ______________________________ Date: ________________

Learning About Vowel Pairs: *Learning About the “ea” Vowel Pair*

Many words have the vowel pair “ea.” The vowel pair “ea” usually makes the long “e” vowel sound. For example, in the word *bean,* the “ea” is sounded as long “e.”

In each of the following sentences you will find a word with the letters “ea.” Read each sentence. Then write the word with the letters “ea” on the blanks in Column I. Write the letters “ea” on the blanks in Column II. On the blank in Column III write the sound that the letters “ea” make.

Sight Words to Know: put do you want are the will room plan going let to in she fell off made

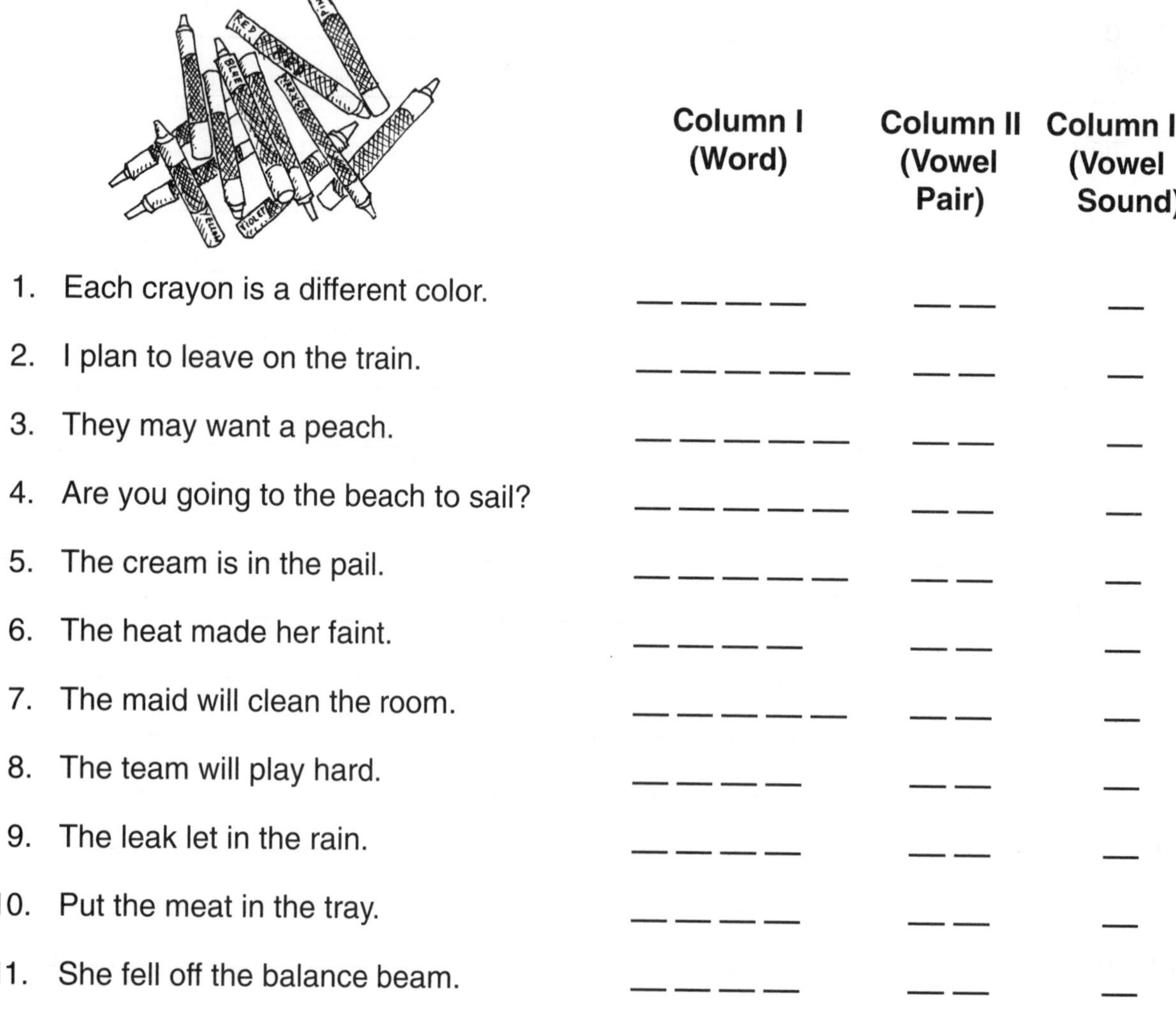

	Column I (Word)	Column II (Vowel Pair)	Column III (Vowel Sound)
1. Each crayon is a different color.	_ _ _ _	_ _	_
2. I plan to leave on the train.	_ _ _ _ _	_ _	_
3. They may want a peach.	_ _ _ _ _	_ _	_
4. Are you going to the beach to sail?	_ _ _ _ _	_ _	_
5. The cream is in the pail.	_ _ _ _ _	_ _	_
6. The heat made her faint.	_ _ _ _	_ _	_
7. The maid will clean the room.	_ _ _ _ _	_ _	_
8. The team will play hard.	_ _ _ _	_ _	_
9. The leak let in the rain.	_ _ _ _	_ _	_
10. Put the meat in the tray.	_ _ _ _	_ _	_
11. She fell off the balance beam.	_ _ _ _	_ _	_
12. The frog made a giant leap.	_ _ _ _	_ _	_

Name: ______________________________ Date: ____________________

Learning About Vowel Pairs: *Learning About the "ea" Vowel Pair*

Place one of the following consonants on the blank to make a word. Write the word on the blanks under Column I. Write the letters that make the long "e" sound on the blanks under Column II. Write a sentence using the word.

s l h m b f p r

	Column I	Column II
1. __eat	__ __ __ __	__ __
Sentence: ______________________		
2. __ean	__ __ __ __	__ __
Sentence: ______________________		
3. __eak	__ __ __ __	__ __
Sentence: ______________________		
4. __eal	__ __ __ __	__ __
Sentence: ______________________		
5. __eam	__ __ __ __	__ __
Sentence: ______________________		
6. __eat	__ __ __ __	__ __
Sentence: ______________________		
7. __eat	__ __ __ __	__ __
Sentence: ______________________		
8. __eam	__ __ __ __	__ __
Sentence: ______________________		
9. __ead	__ __ __ __	__ __
Sentence: ______________________		
10. __eal	__ __ __ __	__ __
Sentence: ______________________		
11. __eak	__ __ __ __	__ __
Sentence: ______________________		
12. __eap	__ __ __ __	__ __
Sentence: ______________________		

Name: ______________________________ Date: ________________

Learning About Vowel Pairs: *Other "ea" Sounds*

You have learned that when a word has the "ea" vowel pair, the long "e" sound is often heard. However, there are many words with "ea" that are pronounced with the short "e" sound. The way the word is used in a sentence often gives a clue to the pronunciation of "ea" words.

Example: "ea" word with long "e" sound = read = I will r**ea**d the paper tomorrow.
"ea" word with short "e" sound = read = I r**ea**d the paper yesterday.

Complete each of the following sentences using one of the words below. Choose a word that completes the meaning of the sentence. Indicate if the word used has a long "e" or short "e" sound.

tread	**beak**	**heavy**	**lead**	**head**
cream	**bread**	**lean**	**ready**	**leak**
leave	**read**	**heave**		

1. We are ______________ to leave for the game. short e __ long e __
2. This meat is very ______________ with little fat. short e __ long e __
3. There is a ______________ in the tire. short e __ long e __
4. I broke the pencil ______________. short e __ long e __
5. You should put a hat on your ______________. short e __ long e __
6. The bag of rocks was too ______________ for me to lift. short e __ long e __
7. That bird has a large ______________. short e __ long e __
8. I ______________ the book for English class. short e __ long e __
9. I will ______________ the book next week. short e __ long e __
10. Can you ______________ the bale to the top of the pile? short e __ long e __
11. She took the ______________ on the second lap. short e __ long e __
12. The ______________ is worn off the tire. short e __ long e __
13. The ice ______________ helped to cool us off. short e __ long e __
14. Make the sandwich with wheat ______________. short e __ long e __
15. Do not ______________ the building until class is over. short e __ long e __

Name: ______________________ Date: ______________

Learning About Vowel Pairs: *Reviewing What Has Been Learned*

Underline the letters that make the long vowel sound in each word. Then write those letters on the blanks in Column I. Finally, write the sound the two letters make on the blank in Column II.

	Word	Column I	Column II
1.	say	__ __	________
2.	leak	__ __	________
3.	claim	__ __	________
4.	eat	__ __	________
5.	way	__ __	________
6.	tray	__ __	________
7.	gain	__ __	________
8.	trail	__ __	________
9.	reach	__ __	________
10.	snail	__ __	________

Use a word from the list on the right to complete the meaning of each sentence.

paid	**wait**
feast	**eagle**
meal	**team**
rain	**cease**
leaf	**peat**
creak	**clay**

1. I will ____________ for you.
2. The ____________ will play to win.
3. The ____________ fell for hours.
4. ____________ is a form of coal.
5. The ____________ flew high in the sky.
6. She ____________ for the ____________.
7. The door opened with a ____________.
8. The pot was made from ____________.
9. She said the food at the ____________ did not ____________ to amaze her.
10. The ____________ fell from the tree to the ground.

Name: ______________________________ Date: ____________________

Learning About Vowel Pairs: *Reviewing What Has Been Learned*

Read the following sentences and complete the blanks.

1. The meal of veal was paid for by the maid.
   (a) The "ea" in *meal* is pronounced as ______________.
   (b) The "ea" in *veal* is pronounced as ______________.
   (c) The "ai" in *maid* is pronounced as ______________.
2. The stain on the rug was gray.
   (a) The "ai" in *stain* is pronounced as ______________.
   (b) The "ay" in *gray* is pronounced as ______________.
3. She will treat the team to a meal of veal.
   (a) The "ea" in *treat* is pronounced as ______________.
   (b) The "ea" in *team* is pronounced as ______________.
4. Each cup of weak tea was cheap.
   (a) The "ea" in *each* is pronounced as ______________.
   (b) The "ea" in *weak* is pronounced as ______________.
   (c) The "ea" in *tea* is pronounced as ______________.
   (d) The "ea" in *cheap* is pronounced as ______________.

5. Please spray the paint on the chain.
   (a) The "ea" in *please* is pronounced as ______________.
   (b) The "ay" in *spray* is pronounced as ______________.
   (c) The "ai" in *paint* is pronounced as ______________.
   (d) The "ai" in *chain* is pronounced as ______________.
6. She is a saint each day.
   (a) The "ai" in *saint* is pronounced as ______________.
   (b) The "ay" in *day* is pronounced as ______________.
7. A heap of grain was on the train.
   (a) The "ea" in *heap* is pronounced as ______________.
   (b) The "ai" in *grain* is pronounced as ______________.
   (c) The "ai" in *train* is pronounced as ______________.

Name: ______________________________ Date: ____________________

Learning About Vowel Pairs: *Learning About the "ee" Vowel Pair*

In each of the following sentences, you will find a word with the letters "ee." When these two letters are together, they make the long sound of the letter "e." Read each sentence. Then write the word with the letters "ee" on the blanks in Column I. Next write the letters "ee" on the blanks in Column II. Finally, on the blank in Column III write the sound that the letters "ee" make.

Sight Words to Know: said, will, cape, need, didn't, meet, she, you, your, at, school, I, well, he, they, my, her

	Column I (Word)	Column II (Vowel Pair)	Column III (Vowel Sound)
1. I will meet you at school.	_ _ _ _	_ _	_
2. You will need your cape.	_ _ _ _	_ _	_
3. She said she will feed the mule.	_ _ _ _	_ _	_
4. He said he didn't feel well.	_ _ _ _	_ _	_
5. The grass is green.	_ _ _ _ _	_ _	_
6. They are going to sleep.	_ _ _ _ _	_ _	_
7. Where are the sheep?	_ _ _ _ _	_ _	_
8. The geese are on the lake.	_ _ _ _ _	_ _	_
9. This is the street where he lives.	_ _ _ _ _ _	_ _	_
10. This water is deep.	_ _ _ _	_ _	_
11. He drove the jeep.	_ _ _ _	_ _	_
12. He is a meek fellow.	_ _ _ _	_ _	_
13. Have you seen her today?	_ _ _ _	_ _	_
14. She gave a good speech.	_ _ _ _ _ _	_ _	_
15. The wheel on my bike is broken.	_ _ _ _ _	_ _	_

Name: ____________________ Date: ____________

Learning About Vowel Pairs: *Learning About the "ee" Vowel Pair*

Place one of the following consonant pairs on the blank to make a word. Write the word on the blanks in Column I. Write the letters that make the long "e" sound on the blanks in Column II. Finally, write a sentence using the word.

sh st bl sl gr str sp fl

	Column I	Column II
1. __ __eet	__ __ __ __ __	__ __
Sentence: ____________________		
2. __ __eet	__ __ __ __ __	__ __
Sentence: ____________________		
3. __ __eet	__ __ __ __ __	__ __
Sentence: ____________________		
4. __ __eed	__ __ __ __ __	__ __
Sentence: ____________________		
5. __ __eece	__ __ __ __ __ __	__ __
Sentence: ____________________		
6. __ __ __eet	__ __ __ __ __ __	__ __
Sentence: ____________________		
7. __ __eeve	__ __ __ __ __ __	__ __
Sentence: ____________________		
8. __ __eed	__ __ __ __ __	__ __
Sentence: ____________________		

Name: ______________________________ Date: ____________________

Learning About Vowel Pairs: *Reviewing "ai," "ay," "ea," and "ee"*

Write the word in the sentence with "ai," "ay," "ea," or "ee" on the blank. Then write the sound the vowel pair makes in that word on the second blank.

	Word	Sound of Vowel Pair
1. The rain was cool on my face.	________	______
2. Her teeth hurt.	________	______
3. I will drink some tea.	________	______
4. He will pay the bill.	________	______
5. They have to read the book.	________	______
6. Is the snow deep?	________	______
7. The food is on the tray.	________	______
8. The beam of light was bright.	________	______
9. He has a small waist.	________	______
10. This sheet of paper is mine.	________	______
11. She did a good deed.	________	______
12. This is the way to town.	________	______
13. Put the water in the pail.	________	______
14. There was a gleam in her eye.	________	______
15. Just stay in bed.	________	______
16. You can walk between us.	________	______
17. Do not let the steam burn you.	________	______
18. Did the train come in on time?	________	______

Name: ______________________________ Date: ____________________

Learning About Vowel Pairs: *Learning About the "oa" Vowel Pair*

In each of the following sentences you will find a word with the letters "oa." When these two letters are together, they make the long sound of the letter "o." Read each sentence. Write the word with the letters "oa" on the blanks in Column I. Then write the letters "oa" on the blanks in Column II. Finally, on the blank in Column III, write the sound that the letters "oa" make.

Sight Words to Know:

	around	was	they	did	he
said	you	could	win	think	will
to	of	this	us	school	sick
man	we	should	have	tell	must
wash	with	don't			

	Column I (Word)	Column II (Vowel Pair)	Column III (Vowel Sound)
1. The goat is eating grass	_ _ _ _	_ _	____
2. The team scored a goal.	_ _ _ _	_ _	____
3. Did he loan you the money?	_ _ _ _	_ _	____
4. Coach said we could win this game.	_ _ _ _ _	_ _	____
5. I think I will have toast.	_ _ _ _ _	_ _	____
6. We will take a boat to the lake.	_ _ _ _	_ _	____
7. I sat in the shade of the oak tree.	_ _ _	_ _	____
8. This road will take us to school.	_ _ _ _	_ _	____
9. Around the castle was a moat.	_ _ _ _	_ _	____
10. They will load the train.	_ _ _ _	_ _	____
11. The sick man began to moan.	_ _ _ _	_ _	____
12. We will have roast for dinner.	_ _ _ _ _	_ _	____
13. She took an oath to tell the truth.	_ _ _ _	_ _	____
14. Wash your hands with soap.	_ _ _ _	_ _	____
15. Don't boast about your victory.	_ _ _ _ _	_ _	____

Name: ______________________________ Date: ____________________

Learning About Vowel Pairs: *Learning About the "oa" Vowel Pair*

Place the following consonants on the blanks to make a word. Write the word on the blanks in Column I. Then write the letters that make the long "o" sound on the blanks in Column II. Finally, write a sentence using the word.

thr c l t gl cl fl r

	Column I	**Column II**
1. __ __oat	__ __ __ __ __	__ __
Sentence: ______________________________		
2. __ __oat	__ __ __ __ __	__ __
Sentence: ______________________________		
3. __oal	__ __ __ __	__ __
Sentence: ______________________________		
4. __oaf	__ __ __ __	__ __
Sentence: ______________________________		
5. __oam	__ __ __ __	__ __
Sentence: ______________________________		
6. __oach	__ __ __ __ __	__ __
Sentence: ______________________________		
7. __oast	__ __ __ __ __	__ __
Sentence: ______________________________		
8. __ __ __oat	__ __ __ __ __ __	__ __
Sentence: ______________________________		
9. __ __oak	__ __ __ __ __	__ __
Sentence: ______________________________		
10. __oast	__ __ __ __ __	__ __
Sentence: ______________________________		

Name: ______________________ Date: ______________

Learning About Vowel Pairs: *Learning About the "ei" Vowel Pair*

In many words that have a vowel combination, the first vowel is given the long sound and the second vowel is silent. However, there are other times when the sound of the vowel combination will depend on the word in which it is found. The best way to determine the sound of these vowel combinations is to determine how the word should be pronounced so that it makes sense in a sentence.

The vowel pair "ei" is found in many words. In the words below, the vowels "ei" will have the long "e" sound as in *either* or the long "a" sound as in *eight.*

Example: **ei**ther = long "e" sound Example: **ei**ght = long "a" sound

In each of the following words, the "ei" vowels have the long sound of "e" or the long sound of "a." Place each of the following words on the correct blank to show the sound of "ei." The first two have been completed for you. On the blank below each word, write a sentence using the word. **Hint:** If you do not know how to pronounce a word, try both the long "e" and long "a" sounds to see if either sound gives a word you know.

	Word	**Long "e"**	**Long "a"**
1.	either	*either*	________
	Sentence: ______________________		
2.	eight	________	*eight*
	Sentence: ______________________		
3.	ceiling	________	________
	Sentence: ______________________		
4.	rein	________	________
	Sentence: ______________________		
5.	freight	________	________
	Sentence: ______________________		
6.	weight	________	________
	Sentence: ______________________		
7.	neither	________	________
	Sentence: ______________________		
8.	neighbor	________	________
	Sentence: ______________________		

Name: ______________________ Date: ______________

Learning About Vowel Pairs: *Learning About the "ie" Vowel Pair*

In each of the following words, the "ie" vowel pair has either the long "i" sound or the long "e" sound. The long sound of "i" is found in the word *die.* The long sound of "e" is found in the word *field.* Place each of the following words on the correct blank to show the sound "ie" makes. The first two have been completed for you. On the blank below each word, write a sentence using the word. **Hint:** If you do not know how to pronounce a word, try both the long "i" and long "e" sounds. See which sound gives a word you know.

	Word	**Long "i"**	**Long "e"**
1.	pie	*pie*	________
	Sentence: ______________________		
2.	field	________	*field*
	Sentence: ______________________		
3.	cried	________	________
	Sentence: ______________________		
4.	fried	________	________
	Sentence: ______________________		
5.	chief	________	________
	Sentence: ______________________		
6.	piece	________	________
	Sentence: ______________________		
7.	tried	________	________
	Sentence: ______________________		
8.	relief	________	________
	Sentence: ______________________		
9.	dried	________	________
	Sentence: ______________________		
10.	shield	________	________
	Sentence: ______________________		

Name: ______________________ Date: ______________

Learning About Vowel Pairs: *Learning About the "ey" Vowel Pair*

In some words, the letter combination "ey" has a long "e" sound. In other words, the "ey" combination makes the long "a" sound.

Example: donk**ey** = long "e" sound **Example:** h**ey** = long "a" sound

Read each of the following sentences and place one of the words from the box below on the blank. Then circle whether that word has a long "e" sound or a long "a" sound. **Hint:** If a word does not make sense using one long sound, try the other long sound.

Sight Words to Know: try, to, find, where, the, have, how, much, do, you, they, with, of, think, must, are, saw, him, that, birds, flew, don't, walk, dark

money	**honey**	**obey**	**covey**	**prey**	**hockey**
they	**alley**	**convey**	**key**	**barley**	**kidney**

1. Open the door with your ____________. long "e" long "a"
2. How much ____________ do you have with you? long "e" long "a"
3. They plan to play a game of ____________. long "e" long "a"
4. Do you think ____________ will be on time? long "e" long "a"
5. We must ____________ the rules. long "e" long "a"
6. They are having ____________ beans for lunch. long "e" long "a"
7. ____________ is a grain similar to wheat. long "e" long "a"
8. Eagles ____________ on mice. long "e" long "a"
9. Please ____________ the message that I will be late. long "e" long "a"
10. ____________ is a sweet substance made by bees. long "e" long "a"

Name: ________________________________ Date: ____________________

Learning About Vowel Pairs: *Reviewing the "ei," "ie," and "ey" Vowel Pairs*

In each of the following sentences is a word that has some letters missing. Complete each word by using one of the vowel pairs "ei," "ie," or "ey." Write long "e," long "i," or long "a" on the blank to show the sound of the vowel pair in the word.

1. The th___ ___f did not want to be caught. Letter pair: ___ ___ Sound: ________
2. They must t___ ___ the rope to the boat. Letter pair: ___ ___ Sound: ________
3. We will rec___ ___ve our money in the mail. Letter pair: ___ ___ Sound: ________
4. I think th___ ___ are coming to the party. Letter pair: ___ ___ Sound: ________
5. That shirt costs too much mon___ ___. Letter pair: ___ ___ Sound: ________
6. N___ ___ther of us will go to the party. Letter pair: ___ ___ Sound: ________
7. They each had a spear and sh___ ___ld. Letter pair: ___ ___ Sound: ________
8. There is the jock___ ___ who rode the horse. Letter pair: ___ ___ Sound: ________
9. The fr___ ___ght train left on time. Letter pair: ___ ___ Sound: ________
10. We will only be there a br___ ___f time. Letter pair: ___ ___ Sound: ________

Below are words with the "ei" and "ie" vowel pairs. Match the words on the right with the definitions on the left. Hint: If you do not know a word, try both vowel sounds to see which sound gives a word you know.

	Definition	**Word**		**Definition**	**Word**
___	1. free time	a. beige	___	6. answered	f. brief
___	2. a color	b. vein	___	7. not the truth	g. thief
___	3. something to ride in	c. deceive	___	8. one who steals	h. replied
___	4. body part	d. leisure	___	9. a piece of land	i. lie
___	5. try to fool	e. sleigh	___	10. short time	j. field

Name: ______________________________ Date: ____________________

Learning About Vowel Pairs That Do Not Give a Long or Short Sound: *Learning About the "oo" Vowel Pair*

The vowel pairs "oo," "au," "aw," and "ew" are found in many words. When these vowel pairs are found in a word, the sound is neither long nor short.

In many words with the vowel pair "oo," the "oo" is sounded like "oo" in *good.* In other words, the "oo" is sounded like the "oo" in *fool.*

Pronounce each of the following words aloud. Listen carefully to how you make the "oo" sound. If the "oo" sounds like the "oo" in *good,* place the word on a blank under **good**. If the "oo" sound like the "oo" in *fool,* place the word on a blank under **fool**.

foot	**pool**	**food**	**brook**	**stood**	**soon**
noon	**book**	**cook**	**hook**	**roof**	**tool**
hood	**wood**	**took**	**loom**	**room**	**broom**
crook	**boot**				

good	**fool**
____________________	____________________
____________________	____________________
____________________	____________________
____________________	____________________
____________________	____________________
____________________	____________________
____________________	____________________
____________________	____________________
____________________	____________________
____________________	____________________
____________________	____________________
____________________	____________________

Name: ______________________________ Date: ____________________

Learning About Vowel Pairs That Do Not Give a Long or Short Sound: *Learning About the "oo" Vowel Pair*

Use one of the following consonants or consonant blends in each blank to make a word that completes the meaning of the sentence.

p z t r b c d f k l br m n

1. I read the __oo__.
2. The ball landed in the __oo__.
3. Did you __oo__ at the pictures?
4. I went to my __oo__.
5. We will __oo__ for the team.
6. Let's stop for some __oo__.
7. We will stop to eat at __oo__.
8. They __oo__ the coat home to Mother.
9. We went to the __oo.
10. She went to wade in the __oo__.

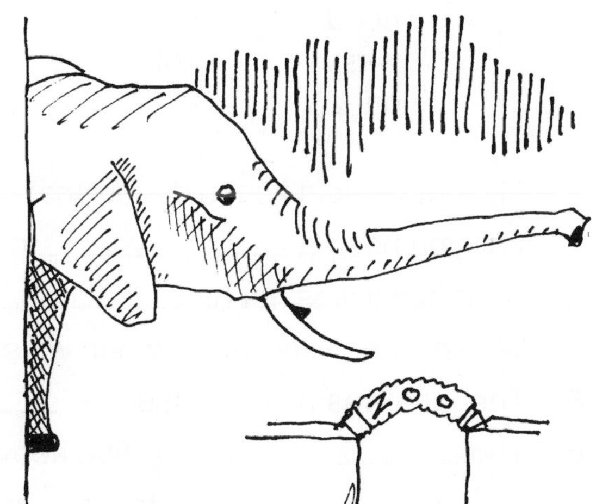

Write a sentence using each of the following words.

1. good: ______________________________
2. mood: ______________________________
3. shook: ______________________________
4. boot: ______________________________
5. stood: ______________________________
6. school: ______________________________
7. hoof: ______________________________
8. tooth: ______________________________
9. wool: ______________________________
10. bloom: ______________________________

Name: ______________________________ Date: ____________________

Learning About Vowel Pairs That Do Not Give a Long or Short Sound: *Learning About the "au" and "aw" Vowel Pairs*

The vowel pairs "au" and "aw" are found in many words. These two vowel pairs both make the sound **/aw/** in words where they are found.

Complete the blank in each sentence below using one of the words with "au" or "aw" from the box at the right.

Sight Words to Know:

	my	said	the	will	you
need	to	your	told	him	it
was	not	we	he	with	some
on	for	they	put	from	in

1. My mother said I should mow the ____________.
2. Will you need a ____________ to drink your soda?
3. I told him it was not his ____________.
4. We knew he was sleepy when we saw him ____________.
5. The food was better with some ____________ on it.
6. The ____________ flew high above the field looking for mice.
7. I ____________ him before the game.
8. They put the money from the game in the ____________.
9. To keep the wind out, put ____________ around your windows.
10. Do not ____________ someone you are angry with.

yawn
vault
sauce
saw
caulk
lawn
assault
straw
fault
hawk

Match the word or phrase in Column II with the correct word in Column I.

	Column I	**Column II**
____	1. brawl	a. baby deer
____	2. dawn	b. opposite of son
____	3. haul	c. a fight
____	4. auto	d. not nice
____	5. jaw	e. part of your body
____	6. fawn	f. a name for a car
____	7. taught	g. just before the sun comes up
____	8. law	h. like a rule
____	9. daughter	i. a truck is used to do this
____	10. naughty	j. something a teacher did yesterday

Name: ______________________________ Date: ______________________

Learning About Vowel Pairs That Do Not Give a Long or Short Sound: *Learning About the "ew" Vowel Pair*

Words to Know: new few

New and ***few*** are rhyming words. Use the letters below to complete the blanks to make other words that rhyme with *new* and *few*. Use the word you have made to make a sentence.

p thr gr kn cr d bl st ch br

1. __ __ew: ______________________________
2. __ __ew: ______________________________
3. __ __ew: ______________________________
4. __ __ew: ______________________________
5. __ __ew: ______________________________
6. __ __ew: ______________________________
7. __ __ew: ______________________________
8. __ __ __ew: ______________________________
9. __ew: ______________________________
10. __ew: ______________________________

Read each of the following sentences. Circle the word in parentheses that best completes the sentence. Then write the word on the blank.

Sight Words to Know: all by day high in the sky long pass

1. The eagle (grew / flew) high in the sky. ____________
2. The wind (blew / stew) all day. ____________
3. I (knew / few) he would be on time. ____________
4. They drove the (chew / new) car. ____________
5. She sat by the lake and (brew / drew) and painted. ____________
6. The hero (slew / grew) the giant. ____________
7. Each ship had a full (crew / mew). ____________
8. She (threw / clew) a long pass. ____________
9. They went to the top of the hill for the (view / new). ____________
10. Mother said she would (hew / brew) the coffee. ____________

Name: ________________________ Date: ______________

Learning About Contractions: *Matching Contractions to Word Pairs*

When you read, you often see words like ***I'll, isn't, we'd,*** and ***won't.*** These words are called contractions. A **contraction** is a short way of writing two words as one.

Examples: **I'll** is a short way of writing **I will**.
Isn't is a short way of writing **is not**.
We'd is a short form of writing **we had** or **we would**.
Won't is a short form of writing **will not**.

In Column I, there are some contractions that you will need to learn to become a better reader. The word pairs on the right match the contractions in Column I. In Column II, place the correct word pair that matches each contraction in Column I.

	Column I	Column II	Word Pairs
1.	I've	________ ________	is not
2.	I'm	________ ________	you are
3.	you'll	________ ________	I have
4.	you're	________ ________	I am
5.	isn't	________ ________	you will
6.	wasn't	________ ________	were not
7.	weren't	________ ________	he will
8.	he'll	________ ________	who is
9.	who's	________ ________	she will
10.	she'll	________ ________	was not
11.	we've	________ ________	will not
12.	we'll	________ ________	they will
13.	they'll	________ ________	we have
14.	won't	________ ________	did not
15.	didn't	________ ________	we will
16.	I'd	________ ________	can not
17.	they've	________ ________	let us
18.	there's	________ ________	I would
19.	let's	________ ________	they have
20.	can't	________ ________	there is

Name: ______________________________ Date: ____________________

Learning About Contractions: *Using Contractions in Sentences*

Use each of the following contractions to make a sentence.

1. we've: ____________________
2. I'd: ____________________
3. they've: ____________________
4. isn't: ____________________
5. I'm: ____________________
6. can't: ____________________
7. there's: ____________________
8. you're: ____________________
9. I've: ____________________
10. he'll: ____________________
11. who's: ____________________
12. won't: ____________________
13. didn't: ____________________
14. he'd: ____________________
15. you'll: ____________________
16. they're: ____________________
17. wasn't: ____________________
18. weren't: ____________________
19. she'll: ____________________
20. you've: ____________________

Name: ______________________ Date: ______________

Learning About Contractions: *Identifying Contractions in Sentences*

Read each of the following sentences. First, circle the contraction in each sentence. Then write the word pair the contraction stands for on the lines in (a). Next, find the words in the sentence indicated by the clues and write those words on the lines provided.

1. I'm not the one who broke the window.
   (a) contraction word pair: __________ __________
   (b) word beginning with a blend, has a long "o" sound and silent "e": __________
2. She'll clean the room.
   (a) contraction word pair: __________ __________
   (b) word beginning with a blend, has a long "e" sound: __________
3. I'll bait the hook.
   (a) contraction word pair: __________ __________
   (b) word with a long "a" sound: __________
   (c) word that rhymes with book: __________
4. Isn't it time to eat the cheese?
   (a) contraction word pair: __________ __________
   (b) word with the long "i" sound and a silent "e": __________
   (c) word with the long "e" sound and a silent "e": __________
5. He'll boast that he won the game.
   (a) contraction word pair: __________ __________
   (b) word with the long "o" sound __________
   (c) word with the long "a" sound and a silent "e": __________
6. Who's the cool guy with the gray wool coat?
   (a) contraction word pair: __________ __________
   (b) word that rhymes with tool: __________
   (c) word with the same "oo" sound as took: __________
   (d) word with the long "a" sound: __________
   (e) word with the long "o" sound: __________
7. They'll need a pail, nail, spade, and rule.
   (a) contraction word pair: __________ __________
   (b) two rhyming words with the long "a" sound: __________ __________
   (c) word with the long "a" sound and a silent "e": __________
   (d) word with the long "u" sound and a silent "e": __________

Name: ______________________________ Date: __________________

Learning About Contractions: *Identifying Contractions in Sentences (continued)*

8. Let's go to the beach and have a feast.
   (a) contraction word pair: __________ __________
   (b) two words with the long "e" sound: __________ __________
   (c) word with the long "o" sound: __________
9. Won't you float in the boat?
   (a) contraction word pair: __________ __________
   (b) word beginning with a consonant blend, has the long "o" sound: __________
   (c) word with the long "o" sound __________
10. We've been to the fudge shop for lunch.
    (a) contraction word pair: __________ __________
    (b) word with the long "e" sound: __________
    (c) words with the short "u" sound: __________ __________
11. You weren't cute in that huge black dress.
    (a) contraction word pair: __________ __________
    (b) words with a long "u" sound and a silent "e": __________ __________
    (c) word beginning with a consonant blend, has the short "a" sound __________
12. I'd like to have a glass of cream and a slab of cheese.
    (a) contraction word pair: __________ __________
    (b) word beginning with a consonant blend, has a short "a" sound: __________
    (c) word beginning with a consonant blend, has a long "e" sound: __________
    (d) word beginning with a consonant blend, had a short "a" sound: __________
13. She'll be mad if the rose is drab.
    (a) contraction word pair: __________ __________
    (b) word beginning with a consonant blend, has a short "a" sound: __________
    (c) word with the long "o" sound, a silent "e," and an "s" that sounds like a "z": ____
14. They'll call the cat and dog for a meal.
    (a) contraction word pair: __________ __________
    (b) words with the short "a" sound: __________ __________
    (c) word with the long "e" sound: __________
15. I didn't think the cost to ride the bus would be fifty cents.
    (a) contraction word pair: __________ __________
    (b) words with the short "i" sound __________ __________
    (c) word with the short "o" and the hard "c" __________

Name: ______________________________ Date: ____________________

Learning About r-Controlled Vowels: *"ar," "er," "ir," "or," and "ur"*

In many words, you find a vowel followed by the letter "r." The **r-controlled** vowel pairs are "ar," "er," "ir," "or," and "ur."

Read each of the following sentences and complete the blank using one of the words in the box on the right.

Sight Words to Know: I, my, in, the, did, you, your, to, pulled, saw, at, of, they, were, that, would, be, on, said, will, come, plan, their, has, very, went, on

1. I broke my ____________ in the game.
2. Did you ride your bicycle to the ____________?
3. The little ____________ pulled the heavy ____________.
4. We saw ____________ at the movie.
5. In the ____________ field was a large ____________ of deer.
6. They were ____________ that they would be on time.
7. He wore a gray ____________ coat.
8. She said to bring a ____________ and some nails.
9. I will come to your house ____________ the game.
10. They plan to ride their ____________ bikes.
11. He has a ____________ with bright colors.
12. She wore a ____________ and blouse to school.
13. A fox has a very smooth coat of ____________.
14. They went to ____________ on Sunday.
15. The ____________ was driving a tractor.

sport
after
arm
church
certain
hammer
corn
dirt
shirt
park
herd
farmer
skirt
burro
cart
her
fur

Name: ______________________________ Date: ____________________

Learning About r-Controlled Vowels: *Writing Sentences*

Write a sentence using each of the following vowel-r words.

1. turkey: ______________________________
2. start: ______________________________
3. person: ______________________________
4. storm: ______________________________
5. bark: ______________________________
6. shore: ______________________________
7. burst: ______________________________
8. purr: ______________________________
9. spark: ______________________________
10. stir: ______________________________
11. curb: ______________________________
12. first: ______________________________
13. barn: ______________________________
14. color: ______________________________
15. fern: ______________________________
16. worm: ______________________________
17. turn: ______________________________
18. warm: ______________________________
19. firm: ______________________________
20. torn: ______________________________

Name: ________________________ Date: ________________

Learning About Consonant Digraphs: *Learning About Words With Beginning Consonant Digraphs "ch"*

Consonant digraphs are two consonant letters that combine to make one sound. The new sound is not a blend of the two letters.

The consonant digraph "ch" may have the sound heard in ***child,*** the sound heard in ***chef,*** or the sound heard in ***chorus.***

Each of the following words begins with the consonant digraph "ch." Pronounce each word and then place it under the heading **Child**, **Chef**, or **Chorus** to indicate what sound the "ch" digraph makes.

chain	chrome	chief	chili	character	chin
cheer	choral	charade	chivalry	chenille	chord
check	choose	cholera	chinook	chemical	chalet

Child	**Chef**	**Chorus**
________	________	________
________	________	________
________	________	________
________	________	________
________	________	________
________	________	________
________	________	________
________	________	________
________	________	________
________	________	________
________	________	________
________	________	________
________	________	________

Name: ________________________ Date: ________________

Learning About Consonant Digraphs: *Learning About Words With Beginning Consonant Digraphs "sh"*

The "sh" consonant digraph is found at the beginning of many words, such as ***ship*** and ***shark***.

Read each of the sentences below and circle the words with the "sh" beginning digraph.

1. He will shut down the ride at nine o'clock.
2. Do you shave every day?
3. The shell contains a shy creature.
4. Shake the box and guess what is inside.
5. The roof will shield us from the rain.

Use the words in the box at the right to complete the sentences below.

shuck
shot
shadow
shed
share
shame
show
she
shark
shore

1. Will you ____________ your candy with me?
2. The great white ____________ has a lot of teeth.
3. Let me ____________ you where to hang your coat.
4. Take the ____________ off the ear of corn before you eat it.
5. Sam can make ____________ puppets with his hands.
6. The wood washed up on the ____________.
7. Her bad behavior caused Lisa some ____________.
8. Frank had to get a ____________ when he had the flu.
9. ____________ will not be back today.
10. Did you put the rake in the ____________?

Name: ______________________ Date: ______________

Learning About Consonant Digraphs: *Learning About Words With Beginning Consonant Digraphs "th"*

The beginning consonant digraph "th" makes two different sounds. In some words, the "th" makes the sound found in ***thing***. In other words, the "th" makes the sound found in ***that***.

Place the following words under the heading **Thing** or **That** to indicate what sound the beginning "th" digraph makes in each word.

those	thread	throw	this	there	thank
the	thought	these	threw	then	thaw

Thing	**That**
______________	______________
______________	______________
______________	______________
______________	______________
______________	______________
______________	______________
______________	______________
______________	______________

Circle the words with the beginning "th" digraph in each of the following sentences.

1. The man threw the ball into the stands.
2. She thought the theme of the story was "love and loss."
3. How can we think with so much noise in this house?
4. This theory explains the reason birds can fly.
5. Is she smarter than those other students?

Name: ______________________________ Date: ____________________

Learning About Consonant Digraphs: *Learning About Words With Ending Consonant Digraphs*

Many words end with a consonant digraph, such as "ch," "ck," "sh," "gh," "lk," and "th." Remember, a consonant digraph is two or more letters that combine to make a new sound.

Each of the words in Column I ends with a consonant digraph. Match the correct meaning from Column II with each word in Column I. Write the consonant digraph on the blanks following the word in Column I.

	Column I Word	Ending Digraph	Column II Definitions
_____	1. beach	__ __	a. opposite of north
_____	2. bench	__ __	b. opposite of smooth
_____	3. clock	__ __	c. opposite of stale
_____	4. sack	__ __	d. sandy area next to the ocean
_____	5. laugh	__ __	e. a subject in school
_____	6. rough	__ __	f. a loud sound
_____	7. dish	__ __	g. used to tell time
_____	8. flock	__ __	h. to say something
_____	9. chalk	__ __	i. what we do when happy
_____	10. fish	__ __	j. used to carry things
_____	11. math	__ __	k. group of sheep
_____	12. south	__ __	l. something to eat
_____	13. fresh	__ __	m. found in a park to sit on
_____	14. talk	__ __	n. something to write with
_____	15. crunch	__ __	o. something to eat on

Name: ______________________________ Date: ____________________

Learning About Consonant Digraphs: *Learning About Words With Ending Consonant Digraphs*

Complete the blanks in each sentence to make a word using the digraphs "ch," "ck," "sh," "lk," "gh," or "th."

1. The beans can be put in the cro__ __ pot.
2. We will need a bru__ __ to paint with.
3. What grade did you get in ma__ __?
4. I hope we cat__ __ some fish.
5. She has a bad cou__ __.

Write the digraph in each word on the blanks by the word. Then write a sentence using each word.

1. each __ __
   Sentence: ______________________________
2. inch __ __
   Sentence: ______________________________
3. luck __ __
   Sentence: ______________________________
4. crash __ __
   Sentence: ______________________________
5. both __ __
   Sentence: ______________________________
6. much __ __
   Sentence: ______________________________
7. enough __ __
   Sentence: ______________________________
8. with __ __
   Sentence: ______________________________
9. rush __ __
   Sentence: ______________________________
10. sick __ __
    Sentence: ______________________________

Name: ______________________________ Date: ____________________

Learning About Consonant Digraphs: *Learning About the Digraph "ph"*

When the consonant digraph **"ph"** is found in a word, it is pronounced as **/f/**. In the word ***phone***, the letters "ph" are pronounced as **/f/**. **Phone** is pronounced as **fone** with a long "o" and a silent "e."

Read each of the following sentences. Find the words with the digraph "ph." Draw a slash through the "ph" and write the word on the blank with the letter "f" replacing the "ph."

Sight Words to Know:	the	is	there	on	table
of	my	if	we	are	going
to	take	second	so	am	his

1. The phone is ringing. ____________
2. There on the table is a photo of my sister. ____________
3. If we are going to play football, we must take a physical. ____________
4. The moon is in the second phase. ____________
5. He is my uncle, so I am his nephew. ____________

In each of the following words, the letters "ph" are pronounced with the sound of "f." Write each word in the **"ph" Deleted** column and place a slash through the "ph." Then write the pronunciation of the word in the **Pronunciation** column. Finally, write a sentence using each "ph" word.

	Word	**"ph" Deleted**	**Pronunciation**
1.	phone	phone	fone
	Sentence: ____________		
2.	phrase	____________	____________
	Sentence: ____________		
3.	nephew	____________	____________
	Sentence: ____________		
4.	graph	____________	____________
	Sentence: ____________		
5.	phonics	____________	____________
	Sentence: ____________		

Name: ______________________ Date: ______________

Learning About Consonant Digraphs: *Learning About the Digraph "gh"*

When the letters **"gh"** come at the end of a word, the "gh" is pronounced as **/f/**. In the word ***laugh,*** the letters "gh" are pronounced as an **/f/** sound. **Laugh** is pronounced as **laf** with the short sound of "a."

Read each of the following sentences. Find the words with the digraph "gh" and draw a line through the "gh." Then write the word on the blank with the letter "f" replacing the "gh."

Sight Words to Know: he, is, will, very, there, guy, cake, from, was, loud, been, sick, on, that, car, road

1. He is a very tough guy. ______________
2. Will there be enough cake for all of us? ______________
3. The laughter from the next room was very loud. ______________
4. He has been sick and has a bad cough. ______________
5. We drove the car on a road that was quite rough. ______________

In each of the following words, the digraph "gh" is pronounced with the sound of "f." Write each word in the **"gh" Deleted** column and draw a slash through the "gh." Then write the pronunciation of the word in the **Pronunciation** column. Finally, write a sentence using each "gh" word.

	Word	"gh" Deleted	Pronunciation
1.	laugh	laugh	laf
	Sentence: ______________		
2.	rough	______	______
	Sentence: ______________		
3.	tough	______	______
	Sentence: ______________		
4.	laughter	______	______
	Sentence: ______________		
5.	enough	______	______
	Sentence: ______________		

Name: ______________________ Date: ______________

Learning About Words With Silent Letters: *Silent "k"*

Many words have letters that are silent. In words that begin with the letters "**kn**," the "**k**" is silent. For example, ***knew*** is pronounced ***new***. The "k" is silent.

In each of the following words, the "k" is silent. Write the word in the **Silent "k"** column and draw a slash through the "k" to show that it is silent. Then write the pronunciation of the word in the **Pronunciation** column. Finally, write a sentence using the word.

	Word	Silent "k"	Pronunciation
1.	knew	k̸new	new
	Sentence:		
2.	knife		
	Sentence:		
3.	knit		
	Sentence:		
4.	knob		
	Sentence:		
5.	knee		
	Sentence:		
6.	knot		
	Sentence:		
7.	knock		
	Sentence:		
8.	kneel		
	Sentence:		
9.	knack		
	Sentence:		
10.	knead		
	Sentence:		

Name: ______________________________ Date: ________________

Learning About Words With Silent Letters: *Silent "gh"*

In some words, the letters **"gh"** are silent. For example, ***night*** is pronounced ***nit*** with a long "i" sound. The "gh" is silent.

In each of the following words, the "gh" is silent. Write the word in the **Silent "gh"** column and draw a slash through the "gh" to show that it is silent. Then write the pronunciation of the word in the **Pronunciation** column, using the macron symbol (¯) for long vowels where appropriate. Finally, write a sentence using the word.

	Word	Silent "gh"	Pronunciation
1.	night	night	nīt
	Sentence: ________________		
2.	light	________	________
	Sentence: ________________		
3.	fight	________	________
	Sentence: ________________		
4.	might	________	________
	Sentence: ________________		
5.	sight	________	________
	Sentence: ________________		
6.	bright	________	________
	Sentence: ________________		
7.	thought	________	________
	Sentence: ________________		
8.	through	________	________
	Sentence: ________________		
9.	brought	________	________
	Sentence: ________________		
10.	caught	________	________
	Sentence: ________________		

Name: ______________________ Date: ______________

Learning About Words With Silent Letters: *Silent "b"*

In words with the letters **"mb,"** the **"b"** is silent. For example, the word ***climb*** is pronounced ***clim*** with a long "i" sound. The "b" is silent.

In each of the following words, the "b" is silent. Write the word in the **Silent "b"** column and draw a slash through the "b" to show that it is silent. Then write the pronunciation of the word in the **Pronunciation** column, using the macron symbol (¯) for long vowels. Finally, write a sentence using the word.

	Word	Silent "b"	Pronunciation
1.	climb	climb̸	clīm
	Sentence: ______________________		
2.	comb	________	________
	Sentence: ______________________		
3.	lamb	________	________
	Sentence: ______________________		
4.	bomb	________	________
	Sentence: ______________________		
5.	dumb	________	________
	Sentence: ______________________		
6.	thumb	________	________
	Sentence: ______________________		
7.	crumb	________	________
	Sentence: ______________________		
8.	bomber	________	________
	Sentence: ______________________		
9.	plumber	________	________
	Sentence: ______________________		
10.	limb	________	________
	Sentence: ______________________		

Name: ______________________ Date: ______________

Learning About Words With Silent Letters: *Silent "c"*

In the some words with the digraph **"ck,"** the **"ck"** is pronounced as **/k/**. The **"c"** is silent. For example, ***black*** is pronounced **blak** with a short "a" sound. The "c" is silent.

In each of the following words, the "c" is silent. Write the word in the **Silent "c"** column and draw a slash through the "c" to show that it is silent. Then write the pronunciation of the word in the **Pronunciation** column. Show the short sound of the vowel by placing the breve (˘) symbol over the vowel. Finally, write a sentence using the word.

	Word	Silent "c"	Pronunciation
1.	black	bla/ck	blăk
	Sentence: ______________		
2.	luck	______	______
	Sentence: ______________		
3.	pack	______	______
	Sentence: ______________		
4.	duck	______	______
	Sentence: ______________		
5.	lock	______	______
	Sentence: ______________		
6.	slick	______	______
	Sentence: ______________		
7.	pick	______	______
	Sentence: ______________		
8.	trick	______	______
	Sentence: ______________		
9.	sack	______	______
	Sentence: ______________		
10.	deck	______	______
	Sentence: ______________		

Name: ______________________ Date: ______________

Learning About Words With Silent Letters: *Silent "w"*

In words with the **"wr"** letter combination, the **"w"** is silent. For example, ***write*** is pronounced as ***rite*** with a long "i" sound. The "w" is silent.

In each of the following words, the "w" is silent. Write the word in the **Silent "w"** column and draw a slash through the "w" to show that it is silent. Then write the pronunciation of the word in the **Pronunciation** column. Use the macron (¯) symbol to indicate a long vowel sound and a breve (˘) symbol to indicate a short vowel sound. If there is a silent "e," draw a slash mark through it. Finally, write a sentence using the word.

	Word	Silent "w"	Pronunciation
1.	write	w̸rite	rīte̸
	Sentence: ______________		
2.	wrote	______	______
	Sentence: ______________		
3.	wrong	______	______
	Sentence: ______________		
4.	wreck	______	______
	Sentence: ______________		
5.	wrap	______	______
	Sentence: ______________		
6.	wrist	______	______
	Sentence: ______________		
7.	wring	______	______
	Sentence: ______________		
8.	wrench	______	______
	Sentence: ______________		
9.	wreath	______	______
	Sentence: ______________		
10.	wren	______	______
	Sentence: ______________		

Name: ______________________________ Date: ____________________

Learning About Words With Silent Letters: *Reviewing What Has Been Learned*

Circle all of the words with silent consonant letters. Then write the words below in the **Words With Silent Letters** column. Finally, write the pronunciation of the words in the **Pronunciation of Words** column.

Sam heard the knock at the door. He looked at the clock and knew it was time to leave for the game. He turned the knob on the door and there stood his friend John with a wrap around his right wrist. In his left hand, John had a sack with a light coat.

"Time to leave for the game," said John.

Sam gave him a knowing smile. "I need to write a note to mother," said Sam.

Sam opened the door again and remembered that there might be a photo after the game, so he would need a comb. He placed the black comb in the pocket of his raincoat.

A light rain began to fall as the game began. It was a tough game with rough play. It took a trick play and a pass that John caught to win the game. Even though he had a cough and a sore thumb, John was able to smile for the photograph.

Words With Silent Letters	Pronunciation of Words	Words With Silent Letters	Pronunciation of Words
____________	____________	____________	____________
____________	____________	____________	____________
____________	____________	____________	____________
____________	____________	____________	____________
____________	____________	____________	____________
____________	____________	____________	____________
____________	____________	____________	____________
____________	____________	____________	____________
____________	____________	____________	____________
____________	____________	____________	____________
____________	____________	____________	____________
____________	____________	____________	____________
____________	____________	____________	____________

Name: ______________________________ Date: ____________________

Learning About Compound Words: *Identifying the Root Words*

In reading, you often find compound words. A **compound word** is a combination of two root words that form a word with a different meaning than either of the root words. For example, words like *inside, baseball,* and *railroad* are compound words.

Compound Word	Root #1	Root #2
inside	in	side
baseball	base	ball
railroad	rail	road

Each of the following words is a compound word. Write the root words on the blanks.

	Compound Word	Root #1	Root #2
1.	houseboat	__________	__________
2.	sidewalk	__________	__________
3.	playground	__________	__________
4.	doghouse	__________	__________
5.	policeman	__________	__________

Each of the following words is a compound word. Write the root words on the blanks, and then write a sentence using the compound word.

		Root #1	Root #2
1.	**cannot**	__________	__________

Sentence: ____

		Root #1	Root #2
2.	**into**	__________	__________

Sentence: ____

		Root #1	Root #2
3.	**however**	__________	__________

Sentence: ____

		Root #1	Root #2
4.	**everybody**	__________	__________

Sentence: ____

		Root #1	Root #2
5.	**without**	__________	__________

Sentence: ____

Name: ______________________________ Date: ____________________

Learning About Compound Words: *Using Compound Words in Sentences*

Complete the blanks in the following sentences by using the compound words from the box below. Write the correct word on the blank.

Sight Words to Know:

he	put	the	in	on
each	of	us	must	take	will
get	can	and	you	some	plan
to	were	by	it	so	

earthquake	**paintbrush**	**suitcase**	**sunset**	**snowman**
fireplace	**campfire**	**afternoon**	**mailbox**	**raincoat**

1. He put the letters in the ________________.
2. Each of us must take a ________________ on the trip.
3. We will get the can of paint, and you can get the ________________.
4. I will get some wood to start a fire in the ________________.
5. We do not plan to leave until late ________________.
6. After the meal, we sat around the ________________ and sang songs.
7. Many buildings were destroyed by the ________________.
8. It looks like rain, so you'd better take your ________________.
9. After the snow stopped, we went out and built a ________________.
10. We sat on the beach and watched the beautiful ________________.

Use each of the following compound words in a sentence.

1. pancake: ____
2. sailboat: ____
3. railroad: ____
4. grandfather: ____
5. moonlight: ____

Name: ______________________ Date: ______________

Learning About Words With Inflectional Endings: *Adding "ing" to Words That End in a Consonant*

An **inflection** is a letter or letters added at the end of a root word that changes the grammatical function of the word. Examples of inflections are "ing," " 's," "es," "s," "ed," "er," and "est."

Many words end with "ing." To add "ing" to words ending with a single consonant, you usually double the last consonant and then add "ing."

Examples: beg = beg**g**ing pat = pat**t**ing

Complete each of the following blanks and make a new word by adding "ing." Write a sentence using the new "ing" word.

	Base Word	Double the Final Consonant	Add "ing" to Make a New Word
1.	run	__ __ __ __	__ __ __ __ __ __ __
	Sentence: ______________		
2.	fan	__ __ __ __	__ __ __ __ __ __ __
	Sentence: ______________		
3.	hit	__ __ __ __	__ __ __ __ __ __ __
	Sentence: ______________		
4.	hop	__ __ __ __	__ __ __ __ __ __ __
	Sentence: ______________		
5.	hug	__ __ __ __	__ __ __ __ __ __ __
	Sentence: ______________		
6.	nag	__ __ __ __	__ __ __ __ __ __ __
	Sentence: ______________		
7.	plan	__ __ __ __ __	__ __ __ __ __ __ __ __
	Sentence: ______________		
8.	jog	__ __ __ __	__ __ __ __ __ __ __
	Sentence: ______________		
9.	pet	__ __ __ __	__ __ __ __ __ __ __
	Sentence: ______________		
10.	shop	__ __ __ __ __	__ __ __ __ __ __ __ __
	Sentence: ______________		

Name: ______________________ Date: ______________

Learning About Words With Inflectional Endings: *Adding "ing" to Words That End in a Silent "e"*

When adding "ing" to a word that ends in a silent "e," first drop the silent "e." Then add "ing" to make the new word.

Example: ride = rid + ing = riding

Complete the blanks below to make a new word ending with "ing." Write a sentence using each new word.

	Base Word	Drop the Silent "e"	Add "ing" to Make a New Word
1.	rake	__ __ __	__ __ __ __ __ __
	Sentence: ______________________		
2.	smile	__ __ __ __	__ __ __ __ __ __ __
	Sentence: ______________________		
3.	take	__ __ __	__ __ __ __ __ __
	Sentence: ______________________		
4.	like	__ __ __	__ __ __ __ __ __
	Sentence: ______________________		
5.	bake	__ __ __	__ __ __ __ __ __
	Sentence: ______________________		
6.	hike	__ __ __	__ __ __ __ __ __
	Sentence: ______________________		
7.	hate	__ __ __	__ __ __ __ __ __
	Sentence: ______________________		
8.	poke	__ __ __	__ __ __ __ __ __
	Sentence: ______________________		
9.	bore	__ __ __	__ __ __ __ __ __
	Sentence: ______________________		
10.	mine	__ __ __	__ __ __ __ __ __
	Sentence: ______________________		

Name: ______________________________ Date: ____________________

Learning About Words With Inflectional Endings: *Reviewing What Has Been Learned*

Complete each of the following sentences by adding "ing" to the words on the right. Write the new "ing" word on the blank in each sentence.

Sight Words to Know:

	other	are	in	were	to
each	the	was	from	they	park
two	their	go	up	is	with
and	our	one	any	did	get
went	come	need	her		

1. He was ______________ swiftly along the beach.
2. We are ______________ in the garden to plant a rose.
3. The boys are ______________ their bikes.
4. They plan to go ______________ up the trail.
5. The boys were ______________ each other about the game.
6. Are they ______________ the tiger?
7. My mother was ______________ the floor.
8. She was in the chair ______________.
9. The sun is ______________ in the east.
10. They were ______________ in the park for exercise.
11. She is always ______________ with her friends.
12. He was ______________ the cake with icing.
13. The two boys were ______________ their mothers for candy.
14. They were ______________ cookies and milk.
15. It looks like our shoes need ______________.
16. They are ______________ for the photo.
17. We were ______________ you could come to the party.
18. The girl was ______________ on one foot.
19. Did you get any new clothes when you went ______________?
20. He was ______________ green beans from the garden.

hop
mop
shine
bug
joke
run
serve
shop
tame
dig
rise
snap
pose
hope
kid
nap
hike
jog
glaze
ride

Name: ______________________ Date: ______________

Learning About Words With Inflectional Endings: *Adding "ing" to Words Ending in "y"*

To add "ing" to words ending with the letter "y," simply add "ing." No changes to the root word are needed.

Examples: fry = frying cry = crying

Complete each of the following blanks and make a new word by adding "ing." Write a sentence using the new "ing" word.

Base Word **Add "ing" to Make the New Word**

1. fly _ _ _ _ _ _
   Sentence: ______________________
2. spy _ _ _ _ _ _
   Sentence: ______________________
3. pay _ _ _ _ _ _
   Sentence: ______________________
4. marry _ _ _ _ _ _ _ _
   Sentence: ______________________
5. try _ _ _ _ _ _
   Sentence: ______________________
6. carry _ _ _ _ _ _ _ _
   Sentence: ______________________
7. copy _ _ _ _ _ _ _
   Sentence: ______________________
8. buy _ _ _ _ _ _
   Sentence: ______________________
9. pry _ _ _ _ _ _
   Sentence: ______________________
10. bury _ _ _ _ _ _ _
    Sentence: ______________________

Name: ______________________________ Date: ____________________

Learning About Words With Inflectional Endings: *Reviewing What Has Been Learned*

Complete each of the following sentences by adding "ing" to the words in the box at the right. Write the correct word on the blank in the sentence.

Sight Words to Know:	the	our	all	us	after
seen	down	their	we	new	to
my	they	are	is	I	am
her	those	fell	during	on	at
was	for	so	true	love	own
sad	she	car	kite		

1. I am ____________ to complete my homework.
2. Is she ____________ for the bike with her own money?
3. We are ____________ a new car.
4. He is ________________ her books.
5. They are ________________ the math problems.
6. They were seen ________________ down the street.
7. All of us are ________________ our English after school.
8. Those ________________ tree limbs fell during the storm.
9. They are planning on ____________ at my house tonight.
10. Are they ________________ the older homes?
11. The girl was so sad she was ____________.
12. Mother is ____________ hamburgers for dinner.
13. The woman is ________________ her true love.
14. Was your brother ____________ on us?
15. He is ____________ a kite.

copy
pay
destroy
marry
study
buy
cry
spy
carry
stay
decay
hurry
fly
try
fry

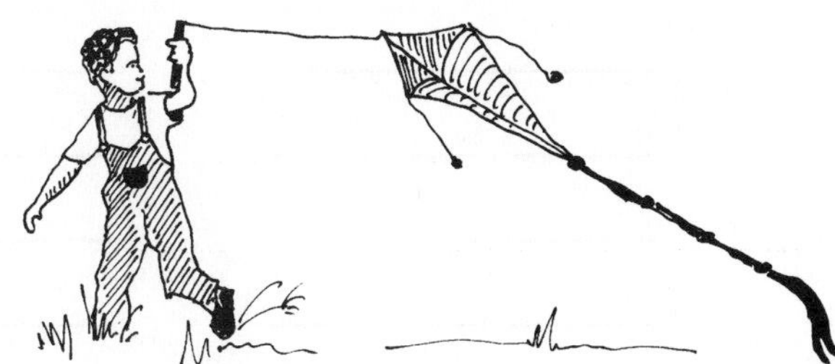

Name: ______________________________ Date: ____________________

Learning About Words With Inflectional Endings: *Adding "s" and "es" to Form Plurals*

The letters "s" or "es" are added to the singular form of a word to make a word plural. **Singular** means "one." **Plural** means "more than one."

Example: kite = singular kites = plural

Each of the following words is either singular or plural. Start with the word *train.* Place it in the appropriate column, **Singular** or **Plural**. Then find its singular or plural match and write it in the appropriate column. Finally, write **s** or **es** on the blank in the **"s" or "es"** column to show how the plural was formed. Cross those two words from the list and continue with the next word pair.

train	books	match	flower	trains	horse
flowers	matches	boy	boxes	eggs	baskets
dish	foxes	basket	dishes	box	cat
pencil	book	brush	cats	shirt	pencils
brushes	shirts	fox	horses	boys	egg

	Singular (one)	Plural (more than one)	"s" or "es"
1.	____________	____________	____________
2.	____________	____________	____________
3.	____________	____________	____________
4.	____________	____________	____________
5.	____________	____________	____________
6.	____________	____________	____________
7.	____________	____________	____________
8.	____________	____________	____________
9.	____________	____________	____________
10.	____________	____________	____________
11.	____________	____________	____________
12.	____________	____________	____________
13.	____________	____________	____________
14.	____________	____________	____________
15.	____________	____________	____________

Name: ______________________ Date: ______________

Learning About Words With Inflectional Endings: *Adding "es" to Words Ending in "y" and "f" or "fe"*

When a word ends in "y" and there is a consonant before the "y," the word is changed to a plural by changing the "y" to an "i" and adding "es."

Example: fly = flies

Change each of the following words in the **Singular Form** column to a word that ends in "ies." Write the new word in the **Plural Form** column.

	Singular Form	Changed to Plural Form by:	Plural Form
1.	fry	dropping the ___ and adding ___ ___ ___	__________
2.	cry	dropping the ___ and adding ___ ___ ___	__________
3.	try	dropping the ___ and adding ___ ___ ___	__________
4.	spy	dropping the ___ and adding ___ ___ ___	__________
5.	penny	dropping the ___ and adding ___ ___ ___	__________
6.	pony	dropping the ___ and adding ___ ___ ___	__________
7.	study	dropping the ___ and adding ___ ___ ___	__________
8.	copy	dropping the ___ and adding ___ ___ ___	__________

To form the plural of words ending in "f" or "fe," change the "f" or "fe" to "v" and add "es."

Examples: wolf = wolves knife = knives

Each of the following words is in the singular form. Complete the blanks for each word and rewrite the word in the **Plural Form** column.

	Singular Form	Changed to Plural Form by:	Plural Form
1.	wolf	change the ___ to ___ and add ___ ___	__________
2.	thief	change the ___ to ___ and add ___ ___	__________
3.	life	change the ___ ___ to ___ and add ___ ___	__________
4.	shelf	change the ___ to ___ and add ___ ___	__________
5.	wife	change the ___ ___ to ___ and add ___ ___	__________
6.	calf	change the ___ to ___ and add ___ ___	__________
7.	leaf	change the ___ to ___ and add ___ ___	__________

Name: ______________________________ Date: ____________________

Learning About Words With Inflectional Endings: *Adding "er" to Words Ending in "y"*

When comparing two things, you may need to change words by adding "er" to the end of the word. When a word ends in "y," change the "y" to an "i" and add "er."

Example: easy = easier

Each of the following words ends in "y." Make a new word by adding "er."

	Word		New Word
1.	dry	change the __ to __ and add __ __ to make	__________
2.	happy	change the __ to __ and add __ __ to make	__________
3.	fancy	change the __ to __ and add __ __ to make	__________
4.	tiny	change the __ to __ and add __ __ to make	__________
5.	funny	change the __ to __ and add __ __ to make	__________
6.	heavy	change the __ to __ and add __ __ to make	__________
7.	muddy	change the __ to __ and add __ __ to make	__________
8.	pretty	change the __ to __ and add __ __ to make	__________
9.	hardy	change the __ to __ and add __ __ to make	__________
10.	rocky	change the __ to __ and add __ __ to make	__________

Change the word in parentheses by adding "er" to make a word that fits the sentence. Write the new word on the blank.

1. She is the (happy) ______________ of the two.
2. This is the (funny) ______________ of the two stories.
3. The large cat is (pretty) ______________ than the small cat.
4. Your boots are (muddy) ______________ than mine.
5. I think math is (easy) ______________ than English.
6. Mums are (hardy) ______________ plants than roses.
7. That big, round rock is (heavy) ______________ than the other one.
8. The bass is (ugly) ______________ than the trout.
9. My brother is (stingy) ______________ than my sister.
10. This road is (rocky) ______________ than the road we drove on yesterday.

Name: ______________________________ Date: ____________________

Learning About Words With Inflectional Endings: *Adding "est" to Words Ending in "y"*

When comparing three or more things, you may need to add "est" to a word. When a word ends in "y," change the "y" to an "i" and add "est."

Example: dry = driest

Each of the following words ends in "y." Make a new word by adding "est." Write a sentence using the new word you have made.

	Word		**New Word**
1.	dry	change the __ to __ and add __ __ __ to make	__________
	Sentence: ______________________________		
2.	happy	change the __ to __ and add __ __ __ to make	__________
	Sentence: ______________________________		
3.	fancy	change the __ to __ and add __ __ __ to make	__________
	Sentence: ______________________________		
4.	tiny	change the __ to __ and add __ __ __ to make	__________
	Sentence: ______________________________		
5.	funny	change the __ to __ and add __ __ __ to make	__________
	Sentence: ______________________________		
6.	heavy	change the __ to __ and add __ __ __ to make	__________
	Sentence: ______________________________		
7.	muddy	change the __ to __ and add __ __ __ to make	__________
	Sentence: ______________________________		
8.	pretty	change the __ to __ and add __ __ __ to make	__________
	Sentence: ______________________________		
9.	hardy	change the __ to __ and add __ __ __ to make	__________
	Sentence: ______________________________		
10.	rocky	change the __ to __ and add __ __ __ to make	__________
	Sentence: ______________________________		

Name: ______________________________ Date: ____________________

Learning About Words With Inflectional Endings: *Reviewing What Has Been Learned*

Change each of the following words to a new word ending in "es."

	Word	New Word With "es" Ending
1.	party	________
2.	quarry	________
3.	ferry	________
4.	query	________
5.	candy	________
6.	dwarf	________
7.	sheaf	________
8.	wharf	________
9.	hoof	________
10.	loaf	________

Change each of the following words to a new word ending in "er" and "est."

	Word	New Word With "er" Ending	New Word With "est" Ending
1.	messy	________	________
2.	fussy	________	________
3.	crazy	________	________
4.	flimsy	________	________
5.	mighty	________	________
6.	squishy	________	________
7.	friendly	________	________
8.	zany	________	________
9.	lazy	________	________
10.	stringy	________	________

Name: ______________________ Date: ______________

Learning About Words With Inflectional Endings: *Adding "s" and "ed" to Make New Words*

Often, new words can be made by adding "s" or "ed" to a word.

Make new words by adding "s" and "ed" to the words in (a) below. Then use each word in a sentence.

1. (a) walk: ______________________
   (b) walk__: ______________________
   (c) walk__ __: ______________________
2. (a) shout: ______________________
   (b) shout__: ______________________
   (c) shout__ __: ______________________
3. (a) wait: ______________________
   (b) wait__: ______________________
   (c) wait__ __: ______________________
4. (a) coast: ______________________
   (b) coast__: ______________________
   (c) coast__ __: ______________________
5. (a) need: ______________________
   (b) need__: ______________________
   (c) need__ __: ______________________
6. (a) land: ______________________
   (b) land__: ______________________
   (c) land__ __: ______________________
7. (a) weed: ______________________
   (b) weed__: ______________________
   (c) weed__ __: ______________________
8. (a) learn: ______________________
   (b) learn__: ______________________
   (c) learn__ __: ______________________

Name: ______________________ Date: ______________

Learning About Words With Inflectional Endings: *Adding "s" and "ed" to Make New Words*

Complete each of the following sentences by using one of the three words following each sentence. Choose the word that makes sense in each sentence and write it on the blank.

1. Yesterday he ____________ the rose in the pot. plant plants planted
2. He will ____________ roses for his mother. plant plants planted
3. She ____________ roses each summer. plant plants planted
4. I ____________ all day for you to call. wait waits waited
5. He ____________ for her each day. wait waits waited
6. If I am late, don't ____________ for me. wait waits waited
7. We had a ____________ at the park. feast feasts feasted
8. Some people have many ____________ each year. feast feasts feasted
9. She said that they ____________ on turkey. feast feasts feasted
10. We ____________ nails all day. pound pounds pounded
11. How many ____________ are in the bag? pound pounds pounded
12. He ate a ____________ of grapes. pound pounds pounded
13. They use wood to ____________ the room. heat heats heated
14. It ____________ up each summer. heat heats heated
15. We had a ____________ talk about the game. heat heats heated
16. Sam ____________ his hair this morning. comb combs combed
17. Her ____________ is pink and blue comb combs combed
18. He ____________ the lawn for weeds every week. comb combs combed
19. We were ____________ in the back of the car. seat seats seated
20. This bus ____________ 48 people. seat seats seated
21. Is this ____________ taken? seat seats seated

Name: ______________________ Date: ______________

Learning About Prefixes and Roots: *"re" and "un"*

A **prefix** is a combination of two or more letters added to the beginning of a root word that changes the meaning of the root word. The prefix **"re"** means "back or again." The prefix **"un"** means "not, lack of, the opposite of, or reverse."

Example: **root** = pay **prefix** = re re + pay = repay means "to pay again"

Each of the following words has the prefix **"re"** or **"un."** Circle the prefix and write the prefix on the blank in the **Prefix** column. The rest of the word is known as the root. Draw a line under the root and write the root on the blank in the **Root** column.

	Word	Prefix	Root
1.	unhappy	_ _	_ _ _ _ _
2.	unsafe	_ _	_ _ _ _
3.	redo	_ _	_ _
4.	unpack	_ _	_ _ _ _
5.	unwind	_ _	_ _ _ _
6.	refill	_ _	_ _ _ _
7.	reopen	_ _	_ _ _ _
8.	unable	_ _	_ _ _ _
9.	uneven	_ _	_ _ _ _
10.	replace	_ _	_ _ _ _ _

In the box on the right is a list of words with the prefixes "re" and "un" that could be used in each sentence to replace the words in bold. Write the correct word on the blank at the end of each sentence.

1. I told him I would **pay** him **back** tomorrow. ______________
2. Coach was **not happy** with the game. ______________
3. She said to **fill** the bottle **again**. ______________
4. The store will **open again** tomorrow. ______________
5. I was **not able** to complete the test. ______________
6. It is **not safe** to swim here. ______________
7. You must **do** the test **again**. ______________
8. The baseball field was **not even**. ______________
9. **Place** the milk in the refrigerator **again**. ______________
10. I am **not like** my sister. ______________

unable
replace
unlike
uneven
repay
redo
unhappy
reopen
refill
unsafe

Name: ______________________________ Date: ____________________

Learning About Prefixes and Roots: *"dis" and "mis"*

Each of the following words has the prefix **"dis"** or **"mis."** The prefix **"dis"** means "away, apart, or to cause to be the opposite of." The prefix **"mis"** means "wrong or not." Circle the prefix and write the prefix on the blank in the **Prefix** column. The rest of the word is known as the root. Draw a line under the root and write the root on the blank in the **Root** column.

	Word	Prefix	Root
1.	distrust	___ ___ ___	___ ___ ___ ___ ___
2.	disable	___ ___ ___	___ ___ ___ ___
3.	misspell	___ ___ ___	___ ___ ___ ___ ___
4.	mislead	___ ___ ___	___ ___ ___ ___
5.	disband	___ ___ ___	___ ___ ___ ___
6.	misshape	___ ___ ___	___ ___ ___ ___ ___
7.	disclose	___ ___ ___	___ ___ ___ ___ ___
8.	dislike	___ ___ ___	___ ___ ___ ___
9.	misfire	___ ___ ___	___ ___ ___ ___
10.	misinform	___ ___ ___	___ ___ ___ ___ ___ ___

In the column at the right is a list of words with the prefixes "dis" and "mis." Match these words with the phrases on the left that could be used in place of the prefix words.

		Phrase	Prefix Word
____	1.	to inform wrongly	a. distrust
____	2.	to not band together	b. disable
____	3.	to lead badly	c. misspell
____	4.	the opposite of like	d. mislead
____	5.	the opposite of close	e. disband
____	6.	to shape wrongly	f. misshape
____	7.	the opposite of able	g. disclose
____	8.	to fire wrongly	h. dislike
____	9.	to not trust	i. misfire
____	10.	to spell wrongly	j. misinform

Name: ______________________ Date: ______________

Learning About Prefixes and Roots: *Reviewing What Has Been Learned*

Combine the root word and the prefix below to make a new word. Write the new word on the blank under **Compound Word**. Next, write a sentence using the root word. Finally, write a sentence using the compound word.

	Root	Prefix	Compound Word
1.	make	re	____________

Sentence (root): ______________________

Sentence (compound): ______________________

	Root	Prefix	Compound Word
2.	place	re	____________

Sentence (root): ______________________

Sentence (compound): ______________________

	Root	Prefix	Compound Word
3.	afraid	un	____________

Sentence (root): ______________________

Sentence (compound): ______________________

	Root	Prefix	Compound Word
4.	tie	un	____________

Sentence (root): ______________________

Sentence (compound): ______________________

	Root	Prefix	Compound Word
5.	agree	dis	____________

Sentence (root): ______________________

Sentence (compound): ______________________

	Root	Prefix	Compound Word
6.	approve	dis	____________

Sentence (root): ______________________

Sentence (compound): ______________________

	Root	Prefix	Compound Word
7.	match	mis	____________

Sentence (root): ______________________

Sentence (compound): ______________________

	Root	Prefix	Compound Word
8.	step	mis	____________

Sentence (root): ______________________

Sentence (compound): ______________________

Name: ______________________ Date: ______________

Learning About Suffixes and Roots: *"ful," "less," and "ly"*

A **suffix** is a combination of two or more letters added to the end of a root word to change the meaning or grammatical function of the root word. The suffix **"ful"** means "full of or having the characteristics of." The suffix **"less"** means "without or not able." The suffix **"ly"** changes a word to an adjective or an adverb and means "characteristic of or in a specified manner, to a specified extent, or at a specified time or place."

Examples:	root = care	suffix = ful	care + ful = careful	"full of care"
	root = glad	suffix = ly	glad + ly = gladly	"in a glad manner"
	root = joy	suffix = less	joy + less = joyless	"without joy"

Add the suffix indicated to each root word below and write the new word in the **New Word** column.

	Root Word	**Suffix**	**New Word**
1.	hope	ful	________
2.	help	ful	________
3.	play	ful	________
4.	cheer	ful	________
5.	use	ful	________
6.	joy	ful	________
7.	hope	less	________
8.	thank	less	________
9.	pain	less	________
10.	help	less	________
11.	use	less	________
12.	clue	less	________
13.	sad	ly	________
14.	kind	ly	________
15.	man	ly	________
16.	loud	ly	________
17.	bad	ly	________
18.	rude	ly	________

Name: ______________________ Date: ______________

Learning About Suffixes and Roots: *Reviewing What Has Been Learned*

Use one of the following words to complete the blank in each sentence. Clues are given after each sentence to help you determine which word would best complete the sentence.

helpless	**loudly**	**playful**	**cheerful**	**useful**	**painless**
hopeless	**joyful**	**kindly**	**helpful**	**rudely**	**thankless**
sadly	**useless**	**manly**	**hopeful**	**clueless**	**badly**

1. The dentist said the cleaning would be ______________. (without pain)
2. The old lady ______________ gave me a cookie. (in a kind manner)
3. The team was so far behind that winning the game was ______________. (without hope)
4. The kitten was in a ______________ mood. (wanted to play)
5. The dog barked ______________. (very loud)
6. The broken glass was ______________ to me. (without use)
7. The hammer was a very ______________ tool. (full of use)
8. She was smiling and ______________ today. (full of cheer)
9. Hunting is a ______________ sport. (characteristic of men)
10. We were ______________ that mother would bring us a treat. (full of hope)
11. When I couldn't get across the street, I felt ______________. (without help)
12. The girl sighed ______________ as she read the story. (in a sad way)
13. Bob was ______________ when he hit a home run. (full of joy)
14. The sleuth was ______________ until he found the fingerprint. (without a clue)
15. I was ______________ awakened at an early hour. (in a rude manner)
16. Making dinner was a ______________ task. (without thanks)
17. Because he refused to practice, Fred played the tuba ______________. (in a bad manner)
18. It was very ______________ to read the directions. (full of help)

Name: ______________________ Date: ______________

Learning About Syllables: *One-Syllable Words*

The number of syllables in a word is determined by the number of vowel sounds heard when a word is pronounced. However, many words have vowel letters that are not heard. If a vowel is not pronounced, it does not make a syllable.

Write the number of vowels seen in each word in the **Vowels Seen** column. Write the number of vowels heard in the **Vowels Heard** column. Then write the vowel sound heard in the **Vowel Sound** column. Each word has **one** syllable. The first one has been completed for you.

	Vowels Seen	**Vowels Heard**	**Vowel Sound**
1. rain	2	1	long a
2. cage	______	______	__________
3. seen	______	______	__________
4. pain	______	______	__________
5. field	______	______	__________
6. team	______	______	__________
7. take	______	______	__________
8. seat	______	______	__________
9. pie	______	______	__________
10. lake	______	______	__________

11. In all of the above one-syllable words

(a) __________ vowels are seen, but only

(b) __________ vowel is heard when the

word is pronounced.

Rule: The number of syllables in a word is determined by the number of vowel sounds heard, not the number of vowels seen.

Name: ______________________________ Date: ____________________

Learning About Syllables: *Two-Syllable Words With the Vowel-Consonant-Vowel Pattern*

Many words have two syllables. When a two-syllable word is pronounced, two vowel sounds are heard.

Example: begin

When a word has a consonant between two vowels (vcv pattern), the word is usually divided after the first vowel. Usually the vowel in the first syllable is long. The vowel in the second syllable is short.

Example: bē/gĭn

Divide each of the following words after the first vowel. Write each syllable on the blanks provided. Read the sentence that follows.

	Word	First Syllable	Vowel (long/short)	Second Syllable	Vowel (long/short/ r-controlled)
1.	begin	be	long	gin	short
	I will **begin** today.				
2.	pilot	________	________	________	________
	The **pilot** flew the plane.				
3.	tiger	________	________	________	________
	We went to the zoo and saw a **tiger**.				
4.	soda	________	________	________	________
	I will drink a **soda**.				
5.	rodent	________	________	________	________
	The rat is a **rodent**.				
6.	paper	________	________	________	________
	Did you bring a pencil and **paper**?				
7.	delay	________	________	________	________
	The rain will **delay** the game.				
8.	music	________	________	________	________
	The **music** was playing on the radio.				

Name: ______________________________ Date: ____________________

Learning About Syllables: *Two-Syllable Words With the Vowel-Consonant-Vowel Pattern*

Some words with the vowel-consonant-vowel (vcv) pattern do not divide into syllables after the first vowel. The word is divided between the consonant and the second vowel. In words like this, the vowel sound of the first syllable is usually the short sound.

Example: The word **robin** has a vcv pattern.
However, the word is divided between the "b" and the "i." rŏb/ĭn

Divide each of the following words into two syllables and complete the blanks. Read the sentence following each word.

	Word	First Syllable	Vowel (long/short)	Second Syllable	Vowel (long/short/ r-controlled)
1.	robin	rob	short	in	short
	The bird is a **robin**.				
2.	money	______	______	______	______
	How much **money** does it cost?				
3.	novel	______	______	______	______
	I read the **novel**.				
4.	rapid	______	______	______	______
	The car was moving at a **rapid** rate.				
5.	linen	______	______	______	______
	The tablecloth was made of **linen**.				
6.	river	______	______	______	______
	We had a picnic by the **river**.				
7.	travel	______	______	______	______
	They plan to **travel** this summer.				
8.	solid	______	______	______	______
	The ice is frozen **solid**.				
9.	honey	______	______	______	______
	Honey is made by bees.				
10.	liver	______	______	______	______
	The **liver** is a large organ in the body.				

Name: ______________________________ Date: ____________________

Learning About Syllables: *Reviewing Two-Syllable Words*

Each of the following words has two syllables. Read each sentence to see how the word is used in the sentence. Divide each word into two syllables. Complete the blanks for each word.

	Word	First Syllable	Vowel (long/short)	Second Syllable	Vowel (long/short/ r-controlled)
1.	comet We saw the **comet** in the night sky.	______	______	______	______
2.	tulip That **tulip** is a pretty flower.	______	______	______	______
3.	final This is your **final** chance.	______	______	______	______
4.	shiver The cold air made me **shiver**.	______	______	______	______
5.	cupid **Cupid** was on the valentine.	______	______	______	______
6.	eager She was **eager** for the game to begin.	______	______	______	______
7.	cement We wrote our names in the **cement**.	______	______	______	______
8.	spider The **spider** built a web.	______	______	______	______
9.	visit I plan to **visit** my friend next week.	______	______	______	______
10.	metal Gold is a soft **metal**.	______	______	______	______
11.	gavel The judge used her **gavel** to call for order.	______	______	______	______
12.	major The storm caused a **major** delay.	______	______	______	______

Name: ______________________________ Date: ________________

Learning About Syllables: *Open and Closed Syllables*

An **open syllable** ends with a vowel sound, and the vowel sound is usually long. A **closed syllable** ends with a consonant sound, and the vowel sound in the syllable is usually short.

Example 1: mu sic The first syllable "mu" is an open syllable because the syllable ends with a vowel. The sound of the vowel "u" is long.

Example 2: mon ey The first syllable "mon" is a closed syllable because the syllable ends with a consonant. The sound of the vowel "o" is short.

The words below are all two-syllable words. Beside each word is a sentence. Read the sentence and then complete the blanks for each word.

1. **comet** We saw the **comet** in the night sky.
   First Syllable: *com* Long or Short: *short* Open or Closed: *closed*
2. **tulip** That **tulip** is a pretty flower.
   First Syllable: ________ Long or Short: ________ Open or Closed: ________
3. **final** This is your **final** chance.
   First Syllable: ________ Long or Short: ________ Open or Closed: ________
4. **shiver** The cold air made me **shiver**.
   First Syllable: ________ Long or Short: ________ Open or Closed: ________
5. **cupid** **Cupid** was on the valentine.
   First Syllable: ________ Long or Short: ________ Open or Closed: ________
6. **eager** She was **eager** for the game to begin.
   First Syllable: ________ Long or Short: ________ Open or Closed: ________
7. **cement** We wrote our names in the **cement**.
   First Syllable: ________ Long or Short: ________ Open or Closed: ________
8. **spider** The **spider** built a web.
   First Syllable: ________ Long or Short: ________ Open or Closed: ________
9. **visit** I plan to **visit** my friend next week.
   First Syllable: ________ Long or Short: ________ Open or Closed: ________
10. **metal** Gold is a soft **metal**.
    First Syllable: ________ Long or Short: ________ Open or Closed: ________

Name: ______________________________ Date: ____________________

Learning About Syllables: *Words That End With a Consonant + "le"*

Many words end with a consonant plus the letters "le." Examples include ti**tle**, ea**gle**, and no**ble**. The final consonant plus the "le" is a separate syllable.

Each of the words below is a two-syllable word ending in a consonant + "le." Complete the blanks for each word. Write a sentence using each word.

	Word	First Syllable	Vowel Sound (long/short)	Second Syllable
1.	title	ti	long	tle
	Sentence: ____________			
2.	eagle	____	____	____
	Sentence: ____________			
3.	noble	____	____	____
	Sentence: ____________			
4.	rattle	____	____	____
	Sentence: ____________			
5.	little	____	____	____
	Sentence: ____________			
6.	fable	____	____	____
	Sentence: ____________			
7.	bridle	____	____	____
	Sentence: ____________			
8.	maple	____	____	____
	Sentence: ____________			
9.	middle	____	____	____
	Sentence: ____________			
10.	bubble	____	____	____
	Sentence: ____________			

Name: ______________________ Date: ______________

Learning About Syllables: *Open and Closed Syllables With the Consonant + "le" Pattern*

In each of the following words, the **consonant + "le"** is a separate syllable. Complete the blanks for each word. Then write a sentence using each word.

	Word	First Syllable	(Open/Closed)	Vowel Sound (long/short)	Second Syllable
1.	cable	______	________	________	______
	Sentence: ________________				
2.	beagle	______	________	________	______
	Sentence: ________________				
3.	bundle	______	________	________	______
	Sentence: ________________				
4.	bugle	______	________	________	______
	Sentence: ________________				
5.	candle	______	________	________	______
	Sentence: ________________				
6.	dimple	______	________	________	______
	Sentence: ________________				
7.	huddle	______	________	________	______
	Sentence: ________________				
8.	idle	______	________	________	______
	Sentence: ________________				
9.	boggle	______	________	________	______
	Sentence: ________________				
10.	spindle	______	________	________	______
	Sentence: ________________				

Glossary of Phonics Terms

Base Word: Often called the root word. Prefixes and suffixes are often added to the base word to make a new word.
base or root = pay
root + prefix = repay
root + suffix = payment

Closed Syllable: A syllable fitting the spelling pattern **consonant-vowel-consonant** (cvc) where the vowel is usually the short sound.
sat pi **lot**

Consonant Blends: The consonant blends are two- or three-letter combinations like "bl," "gl," "st," and "scr." When these letter combinations are found in a word, the sounds of the letters are all heard when pronouncing the word. The consonant blend combinations are usually found at the beginning or end of a word.

Consonant Digraphs: Consonant combinations like "ph," "ch," "gh," "th," "sh," and "ng." When pronounced, these consonant combinations make a sound that is unlike the sounds of the letters that make up the combination.

Consonants: All of the letters of the alphabet except "a," "e," "i," "o," and "u"

Contractions: Words from which one or more letters have been omitted and an apostrophe is used to take the place of the missing letters. **isn't = is not**
there's = there is

Inflections: A letter or letters added at the end of a root word that changes the grammatical function of the word.
's = inflection to indicate possession (boy's)
s = inflection to indicate plural (boys)
ed = inflection to indicate past tense (jumped)
er = inflection to indicate comparison of two things (faster)
est = inflection to indicate comparison of three or more things (fastest)

Long Vowel Sounds: The name of the vowel is the long sound. It is marked with the macron symbol (¯) over the vowel.

Onset: The part of the syllable that comes before the vowel in a word or syllable.
cat = **c** at
The onset is **c** and the rime is **at**.

Open Syllable: A syllable fitting the **consonant-vowel** (cv) spelling pattern where the vowel is usually the long sound.
go **pi** lot

Prefixes: One or more letter combinations added at the beginning of a base word that changes the meaning of the word. **pay** (base word)
re (prefix)
repay (prefix and base word)

Rime: The part of the syllable that comes after the consonant in a word or syllable.
spring = spr **ing**
The onset is **spr** and the rime is **ing**.

Glossary of Phonics Terms

Short Vowel Sounds: The sounds of the vowel in the words **bat**, **bit**, **met**, **pot**, and **nut**. The short sound is marked with the breve (˘) over the vowel.

Sight Words to Know: Words the student can pronounce as sight words without using phonics or contextual skills. In the exercises in this book, students should know these words as sight words to gain maximum benefit from phonics instruction.

Suffixes: One or more letter combinations added at the end of a base word that changes the meaning or grammatical function of the word.
pay (base word)
ment (suffix)
payment (base word and suffix)

Syllable: A vowel or vowel and other letters that form a pronounceable unit in a word. A syllable must have a vowel that is heard when the word is pronounced.

The Consonant "c": The consonant "c" has a hard and a soft sound. The soft sound of "c" is the sound in **cent** and **fence**. The hard sound of "c" is the sound in **cat** and **call**.

The Consonant "g": The consonant "g" has a hard and a soft sound. The hard sound of "g" is the sound heard in **go** and **got**. The soft sound of "g" is the sound heard in **gym**.

The Consonant "s": The consonant "s" can have the soft sound heard in **see** or the hard sound heard in **rose**.

Vowel Diphthong: Pairs of vowels like "oi," "oy," and "ou." These vowel pairs make a gliding sound when pronounced.

Vowel-r Combinations: The special sound of the vowels when followed by the letter "r."
far, **fir**, **for**, **fur**, **herd**

Vowels: The letters "a," "e," "i," "o," and "u" and in special situations, the consonants "w" and "y"

"y" as a Consonant or Vowel: The letter "y" is a consonant sound when it is at the beginning of a word or syllable. The letter "y" has the vowel sound of long "a," long "e," or long "i" when it is at the end of a word or syllable.
funny, **day**, **sky**

Name: ______________________ Date: ______________

Learning About Consonants: *Consonants in the Beginning Position*

Sight Words to Know: there, was, who, had, and, from, ate, more, than, by, pets, down, street, in, were, they

Place one of the following consonants on the blanks to form a word that makes sense in the stories.

c d m f p t

1. There was a m an who had t wo p ets. He had a c at and a d og. The m an f ed the c at and d og m ilk from a p an.

c d m

2. The C at ate more m ilk than the d og.

p t s m

3. The t wo p ets S at by the m an.

two five

4. There was a man who had a cat and dog. He had two pets.

g r b

5. A b oy and g irl r an down the street.

b g c

6. The b oy kicked a c an, and the g irl carried a b ag.

c d b p h

7. In the b ag were two h ot d ogs and a c an of soda p op.

p k r

8. The K ids stopped to r est at the p ark.

s f l

9. They S at on a l og and ate the f ood.

Name: ______________________ Date: ______________

Learning About Consonants: *Making Words With Consonants in the Beginning Position*

Make a new word by placing the consonant on the blank. Write the word you have made on the three blanks. Write a sentence using the new word you have made.

s
1. S at sat
Sentence: will vary

b
2. b at bat
Sentence: ____________

p
3. p it pit
Sentence: ____________

f
4. f it fit
Sentence: ____________

h
5. h ot hot
Sentence: ____________

c
6. C ot cot
Sentence: ____________

l
7. l et let
Sentence: ____________

r
8. r ut rut
Sentence: ____________

Name: ______________________ Date: ______________

Learning About Consonants: *Making Words With Consonants in the Beginning Position*

Make a new word by placing the consonant on the blank. Write the word you have made on the three blanks. Write a sentence using the new word you have made.

r
1. r at rat
Sentence: will vary

h
2. h it hit
Sentence: ____________

s
3. S et set
Sentence: ____________

b
4. b og bog
Sentence: ____________

l
5. l ot lot
Sentence: ____________

p
6. p en pen
Sentence: ____________

c
7. C ut cut
Sentence: ____________

b
8. b ut but
Sentence: ____________

Name: ______________________ Date: ______________

Learning About Consonants: *Making Words With Consonants in the Beginning Position*

Make a new word by placing the consonant on the blank. Write the word you have made on the three blanks. Write a sentence using the new word you have made.

d
1. d og dog
Sentence: will vary

n
2. n ut nut
Sentence: ____________

m
3. m ap map
Sentence: ____________

s
4. S it sit
Sentence: ____________

n
5. n ot not
Sentence: ____________

s
6. S ad sad
Sentence: ____________

m
7. m en men
Sentence: ____________

MAP SAD

Phonics and Vocabulary Skills: Grade 4 — Making Words With Consonants in the Ending Position

Name: ______________________ Date: ______________

Learning About Consonants: *Making Words With Consonants in the Ending Position*

Make a new word by placing the consonant on the blank at the end of each word. Write the word you have made on the three blanks. Write a sentence using the new word you have made.

t
1. sa<u>t</u> <u>s a t</u>
Sentence: <u>will vary</u>

g
2. sa<u>g</u> <u>s a g</u>
Sentence: ______________

t
3. ma<u>t</u> <u>m a t</u>
Sentence: ______________

d
4. ma<u>d</u> <u>m a d</u>
Sentence: ______________

p
5. ma<u>p</u> <u>m a p</u>
Sentence: ______________

n
6. fu<u>n</u> <u>f u n</u>
Sentence: ______________

d
7. be<u>d</u> <u>b e d</u>
Sentence: ______________

n
8. pi<u>n</u> <u>p i n</u>
Sentence: ______________

© Mark Twain Media, Inc., Publisher 5

Phonics and Vocabulary Skills: Grade 4 — Making Words With Consonants in the Ending Position

Name: ______________________ Date: ______________

Learning About Consonants: *Making Words With Consonants in the Ending Position*

Make a new word by placing the consonant on the blank at the end of each word. Write the word you have made on the three blanks. Write a sentence using the new word you have made.

w
1. sa<u>w</u> <u>s a w</u>
Sentence: <u>will vary</u>

n
2. ra<u>n</u> <u>r a n</u>
Sentence: ______________

g
3. be<u>g</u> <u>b e g</u>
Sentence: ______________

b
4. da<u>b</u> <u>d a b</u>
Sentence: ______________

t
5. pi<u>t</u> <u>p i t</u>
Sentence: ______________

y
6. da<u>y</u> <u>d a y</u>
Sentence: ______________

b
7. ca<u>b</u> <u>c a b</u>
Sentence: ______________

g
8. ho<u>g</u> <u>h o g</u>
Sentence: ______________

© Mark Twain Media, Inc., Publisher 6

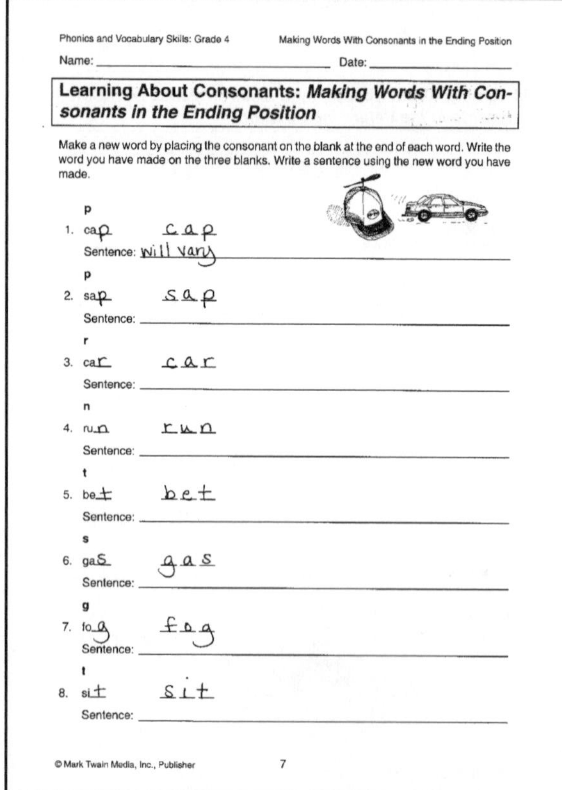

Phonics and Vocabulary Skills: Grade 4 — Making Words With Consonants in the Ending Position

Name: ______________________ Date: ______________

Learning About Consonants: *Making Words With Consonants in the Ending Position*

Make a new word by placing the consonant on the blank at the end of each word. Write the word you have made on the three blanks. Write a sentence using the new word you have made.

p
1. ca<u>p</u> <u>c a p</u>
Sentence: <u>will vary</u>

p
2. sa<u>p</u> <u>s a p</u>
Sentence: ______________

r
3. ca<u>r</u> <u>c a r</u>
Sentence: ______________

n
4. ru<u>n</u> <u>r u n</u>
Sentence: ______________

t
5. be<u>t</u> <u>b e t</u>
Sentence: ______________

s
6. ga<u>s</u> <u>g a s</u>
Sentence: ______________

g
7. fo<u>g</u> <u>f o g</u>
Sentence: ______________

t
8. si<u>t</u> <u>s i t</u>
Sentence: ______________

© Mark Twain Media, Inc., Publisher 7

Phonics and Vocabulary Skills: Grade 4 — The Special Sounds of the Consonant "c"

Name: ______________________ Date: ______________

Learning About Consonants: *The Special Sounds of the Consonant "c"*

The consonants "c," "g," and "s" are special consonants. The sound of each of these consonants depends on the letter that follows the "c," "g," or "s" in a word.

The Consonant "c"

1. When the consonant "c" is followed by the letters "a," "o," or "u," the "c" is pronounced as /k/. Example: The "c" in *cat* is pronounced as /k/.
2. When the consonant "c" is followed by the letters "i" or "e," the "c" is pronounced as /s/. Example: The "c" in *city* is pronounced as /s/.

The Hard and Soft Sounds of "c"

The consonant "c" says /k/ in words like *cat*. This is the hard sound of "c." The consonant "c" says /s/ in words like *cent*. This is the soft sound of "c." Pronounce each of the following words and place the letter /s/ or /k/ on the blank in the following sentences to show which sound the consonant "c" is making in that word.

Sight Words to Know: city, is, twenty, cold, corn, the, I, drank, live, milk, in, it, has

1. The cat drank the milk. /<u>K</u>/ cat
2. It is cold. /<u>K</u>/ cold
3. I live in the city. /<u>S</u>/ city
4. He has twenty cents. /<u>S</u>/ cents
5. The horse ate the corn. /<u>K</u>/ corn
6. She can run fast. /<u>K</u>/ can
7. A plant cell is alive. /<u>S</u>/ cell
8. Cut the pizza in half. /<u>K</u>/ cut

Place the letter **k** or **s** on the blank before each of the following words to show how the consonant "c" is sounded.

1. <u>S</u> city	2. <u>S</u> cider	3. <u>K</u> came	4. <u>S</u> cinder
5. <u>K</u> come	6. <u>K</u> cost	7. <u>S</u> center	8. <u>S</u> cell
9. <u>K</u> cake	10. <u>K</u> coke	11. <u>K</u> cane	12. <u>K</u> cut

© Mark Twain Media, Inc., Publisher 8

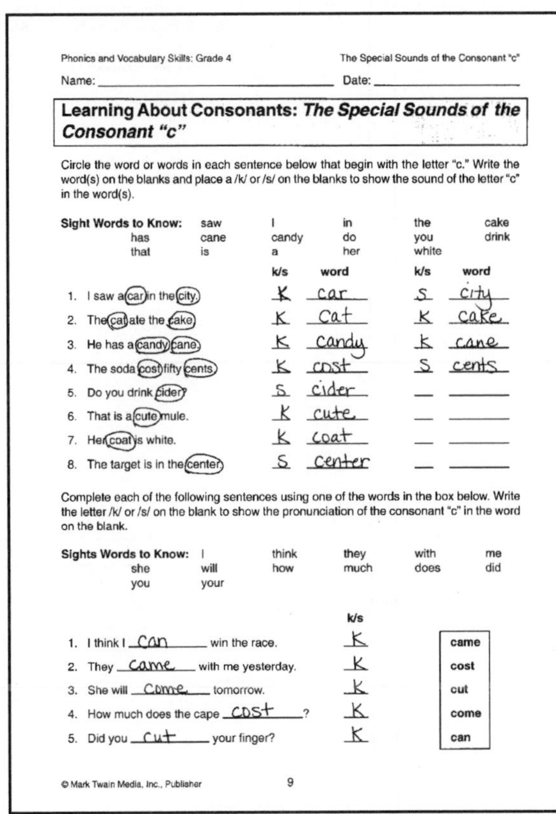

Phonics and Vocabulary Skills: Grade 4 The Special Sounds of the Consonant "c"

Name: ____________ Date: ____________

Learning About Consonants: *The Special Sounds of the Consonant "c"*

Circle the word or words in each sentence below that begin with the letter "c." Write the word(s) on the blanks and place a /k/ or /s/ on the blanks to show the sound of the letter "c" in the word(s).

Sight Words to Know: saw, I, in, the, cake, has, cane, candy, do, you, drink, that, is, a, her, white

	k/s	word	k/s	word
1. I saw a (car) in the (city).	k	car	s	city
2. The (cat) ate the (cake).	k	cat	k	cake
3. He has a (candy) (cane).	k	candy	k	cane
4. The soda (cost) fifty (cents).	k	cost	s	cents
5. Do you drink (cider)?	s	cider	___	___
6. That is a (cute) mule.	k	cute	___	___
7. Her (coat) is white.	k	coat	___	___
8. The target is in the (center).	s	center	___	___

Complete each of the following sentences using one of the words in the box below. Write the letter /k/ or /s/ on the blank to show the pronunciation of the consonant "c" in the word on the blank.

Sights Words to Know: I, think, they, with, me, she, will, how, much, does, did, you, your

	k/s
1. I think I can win the race.	k
2. They came with me yesterday.	k
3. She will come tomorrow.	k
4. How much does the cape cost?	k
5. Did you cut your finger?	k

Word box: came, cost, cut, come, can

© Mark Twain Media, Inc., Publisher 9

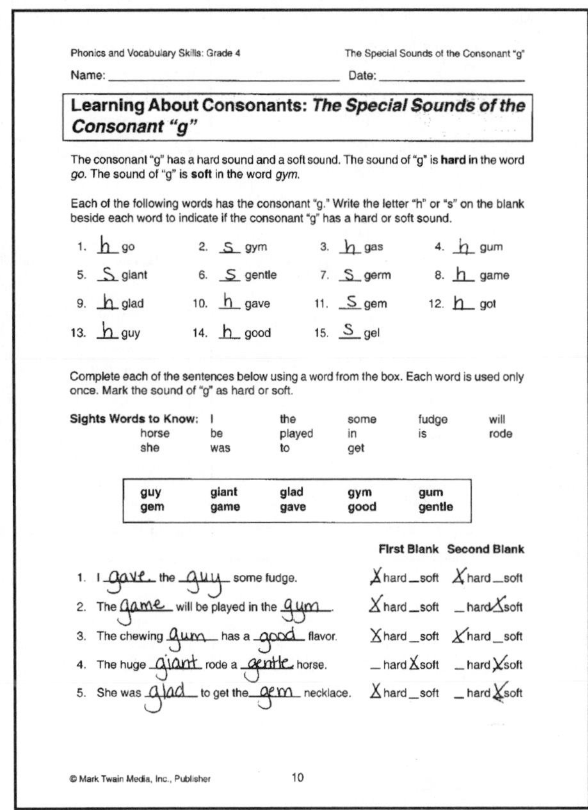

Phonics and Vocabulary Skills: Grade 4 The Special Sounds of the Consonant "g"

Name: ____________ Date: ____________

Learning About Consonants: *The Special Sounds of the Consonant "g"*

The consonant "g" has a hard sound and a soft sound. The sound of "g" is **hard** in the word *go*. The sound of "g" is **soft** in the word *gym*.

Each of the following words has the consonant "g." Write the letter "h" or "s" on the blank beside each word to indicate if the consonant "g" has a hard or soft sound.

1. h go 2. s gym 3. h gas 4. h gum
5. s giant 6. s gentle 7. s germ 8. h game
9. h glad 10. h gave 11. s gem 12. h got
13. h guy 14. h good 15. s gel

Complete each of the sentences below using a word from the box. Each word is used only once. Mark the sound of "g" as hard or soft.

Sights Words to Know: I, the, some, fudge, will, horse, be, played, in, is, rode, she, was, to, get

guy	giant	glad	gym	gum
gem	game	gave	good	gentle

	First Blank	Second Blank
1. I gave the guy some fudge.	X hard ___ soft	X hard ___ soft
2. The game will be played in the gym.	X hard ___ soft	___ hard X soft
3. The chewing gum has a good flavor.	X hard ___ soft	X hard ___ soft
4. The huge giant rode a gentle horse.	___ hard X soft	___ hard X soft
5. She was glad to get the gem necklace.	X hard ___ soft	___ hard X soft

© Mark Twain Media, Inc., Publisher 10

Phonics and Vocabulary Skills: Grade 4 The Special Sounds of the Consonant "s"

Name: ____________ Date: ____________

Learning About Consonants: *The Special Sounds of the Consonant "s"*

In the following words, the letter "s" has either the soft sound of /s/ or the hard sound of /z/. Place an /s/ or /z/ on the blank before each word to indicate if the sound is /s/ or /z/.

1. s sit 2. z his 3. s side 4. s so
5. z rose 6. s us 7. s send 8. s sun
9. s sad 10. s see 11. s said 12. s gust
13. s gas 14. z busy 15. z rise

Complete each sentence below by using the words in the box. On the blank, indicate if the sound of "s" is /s/ or /z/.

Sight Words to Know: I, will, a, he, would, be, home, letter, of, fudge, soon, flower, very, she, when, sky, clear, for, many, miles, has, long

nose	rose	soap	send	noise
see	sand	his	said	sad

	/s/	/z/
1. I will send a letter.	X	___
2. He said he would be home soon.	X	___
3. The box of fudge is his.	___	X
4. The rose is a flower.	___	X
5. She looks very sad.	X	___
6. When the sky is clear, I can see for many miles.	X	___
7. The animal has a long nose.	___	X
8. Wash your hands with soap.	X	___
9. The sand on the beach is warm.	X	___
10. Did you hear that noise?	___	X

© Mark Twain Media, Inc., Publisher 11

Phonics and Vocabulary Skills: Grade 4 Reviewing the Sounds of "c," "g," and "s"

Name: ____________ Date: ____________

Learning About Consonants: *Reviewing the Sounds of "c," "g," and "s"*

Pronounce each of the following words. Place a check mark on the blank to show the sound the consonant in bold makes. Write a sentence using the word.

1. cut X /k/ ___ /s/
Sentence: Will vary
2. gym ___ hard X soft
Sentence: ____________
3. come X /k/ ___ /s/
Sentence: ____________
4. cent ___ /k/ X /s/
Sentence: ____________
5. gone X hard ___ soft
Sentence: ____________
6. his ___ /s/ X /z/
Sentence: ____________
7. sad X /s/ ___ /z/
Sentence: ____________
8. call X /k/ ___ /s/
Sentence: ____________
9. rose ___ /s/ X /z/
Sentence: ____________
10. gem ___ hard X soft
Sentence: ____________

© Mark Twain Media, Inc., Publisher 12

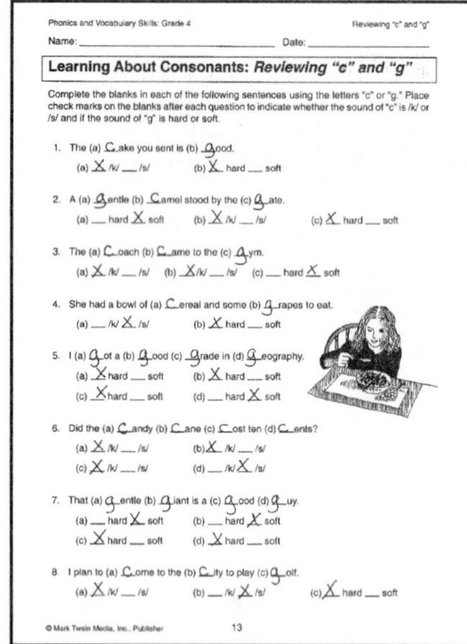

Phonics and Vocabulary Skills: Grade 4 Reviewing "c" and "g"

Name: ______________________ Date: ______________

Learning About Consonants: ***Reviewing "c" and "g"***

Complete the blanks in each of the following sentences using the letters "c" or "g." Place check marks on the blanks after each question to indicate whether the sound of "c" is /k/ or /s/ and if the sound of "g" is hard or soft.

1. The (a) c ake you sent is (b) g ood.
   (a) X /k/ __ /s/ (b) X hard __ soft
2. A (a) g entle (b) c amel stood by the (c) g ate.
   (a) __ hard X soft (b) X /k/ __ /s/ (c) X hard __ soft
3. The (a) c oach (b) c ame to the (c) g ym.
   (a) X /k/ __ /s/ (b) X /k/ __ /s/ (c) __ hard X soft
4. She had a bowl of (a) c ereal and some (b) g rapes to eat.
   (a) __ /k/ X /s/ (b) X hard __ soft
5. I (a) g ot a (b) g ood (c) g rade in (d) g eography.
   (a) X hard __ soft (b) X hard __ soft
   (c) X hard __ soft (d) __ hard X soft
6. Did the (a) c andy (b) c ane (c) c ost ten (d) c ents?
   (a) X /k/ __ /s/ (b) X /k/ __ /s/
   (c) X /k/ __ /s/ (d) __ /k/ X /s/
7. That (a) g entle (b) g iant is a (c) g ood (d) g uy.
   (a) __ hard X soft (b) __ hard X soft
   (c) X hard __ soft (d) X hard __ soft
8. I plan to (a) c ome to the (b) c ity to play (c) g olf.
   (a) X /k/ __ /s/ (b) __ /k/ X /s/ (c) X hard __ soft

© Mark Twain Media, Inc., Publisher 13

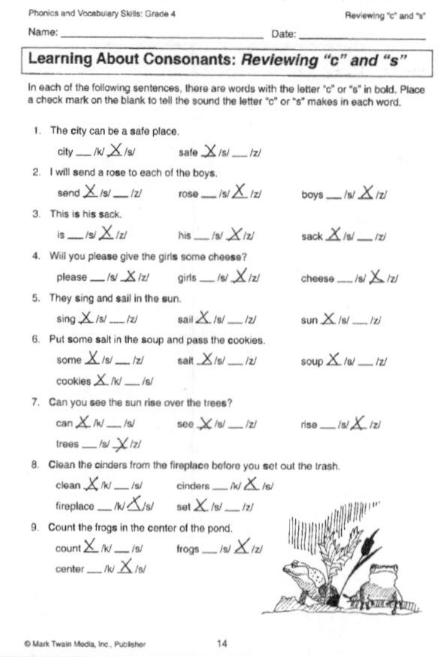

Phonics and Vocabulary Skills: Grade 4 Reviewing "c" and "s"

Name: ______________________ Date: ______________

Learning About Consonants: ***Reviewing "c" and "s"***

In each of the following sentences, there are words with the letter "c" or "s" in bold. Place a check mark on the blank to tell the sound the letter "c" or "s" makes in each word.

1. The **c**ity can be a **s**afe place.
   city __ /k/ X /s/ safe X /s/ __ /z/
2. I will **s**end a ro**s**e to each of the boy**s**.
   send X /s/ __ /z/ rose __ /s/ X /z/ boys __ /s/ X /z/
3. This i**s** hi**s** **s**ack.
   is __ /s/ X /z/ his __ /s/ X /z/ sack X /s/ __ /z/
4. Will you plea**s**e give the girl**s** some chee**s**e?
   please __ /s/ X /z/ girls __ /s/ X /z/ cheese __ /s/ X /z/
5. They **s**ing and **s**ail in the **s**un.
   sing X /s/ __ /z/ sail X /s/ __ /z/ sun X /s/ __ /z/
6. Put **s**ome **s**alt in the **s**oup and pass the **c**ookies.
   some X /s/ __ /z/ salt X /s/ __ /z/ soup X /s/ __ /z/
   cookies X /k/ __ /s/
7. **C**an you **s**ee the sun ri**s**e over the tree**s**?
   can X /k/ __ /s/ see X /s/ __ /z/ rise __ /s/ X /z/
   trees __ /s/ X /z/
8. **C**lean the **c**inders from the firepla**c**e before you **s**et out the trash.
   clean X /k/ __ /s/ cinders __ /k/ X /s/
   fireplace __ /k/ X /s/ set X /s/ __ /z/
9. **C**ount the frog**s** in the **c**enter of the pond.
   count X /k/ __ /s/ frogs __ /s/ X /z/
   center __ /k/ X /s/

© Mark Twain Media, Inc., Publisher 14

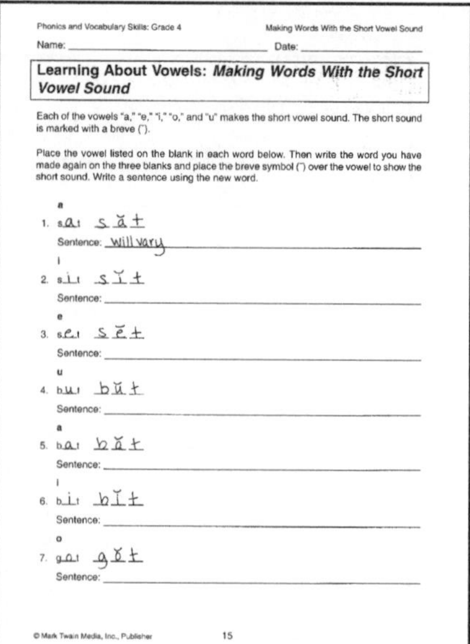

Phonics and Vocabulary Skills: Grade 4 Making Words With the Short Vowel Sound

Name: ______________________ Date: ______________

Learning About Vowels: ***Making Words With the Short Vowel Sound***

Each of the vowels "a," "e," "i," "o," and "u" makes the short vowel sound. The short sound is marked with a breve (˘).

Place the vowel listed on the blank in each word below. Then write the word you have made again on the three blanks and place the breve symbol (˘) over the vowel to show the short sound. Write a sentence using the new word.

1. (a) s a t — s ă t
   Sentence: will vary
2. (i) s i t — s ĭ t
   Sentence:
3. (e) s e t — s ĕ t
   Sentence:
4. (u) b u t — b ŭ t
   Sentence:
5. (a) b a t — b ă t
   Sentence:
6. (i) b i t — b ĭ t
   Sentence:
7. (o) g o t — g ŏ t
   Sentence:

© Mark Twain Media, Inc., Publisher 15

Phonics and Vocabulary Skills: Grade 4 Making Words With the Short Vowel Sound

Name: ______________________ Date: ______________

Learning About Vowels: ***Making Words With the Short Vowel Sound***

Place the vowel listed on the blank in each word below. Then write the word you have made again on the three blanks and place the breve symbol (˘) over the vowel to show the short sound. Write a sentence using the new word.

1. (a) m a t — m ă t
   Sentence: will vary
2. (e) m e t — m ĕ t
   Sentence:
3. (u) r u t — r ŭ t
   Sentence:
4. (o) r o t — r ŏ t
   Sentence:
5. (i) t i n — t ĭ n
   Sentence:
6. (o) t o n — t ŏ n
   Sentence:
7. (a) t a n — t ă n
   Sentence:
8. (u) f u n — f ŭ n
   Sentence:

© Mark Twain Media, Inc., Publisher 16

Phonics and Vocabulary Skills: Grade 4 Making Words With the Short Vowel Sound

Name: ______________________ Date: ______________

Learning About Vowels: ***Making Words With the Short Vowel Sound***

Place the vowel listed on the blank in each word below. Then write the word you have made again on the three blanks and place the breve symbol (˘) over the vowel to show the short sound. Write a sentence using the new word.

1. (a) f a n — f ă n
   Sentence: will vary
2. (i) f i n — f ĭ n
   Sentence:
3. (u) p u n — p ŭ n
   Sentence:
4. (a) p a n — p ă n
   Sentence:
5. (i) p i n — p ĭ n
   Sentence:
6. (e) d e n — d ĕ n
   Sentence:
7. (o) n o t — n ŏ t
   Sentence:
8. (u) n u t — n ŭ t
   Sentence:

© Mark Twain Media, Inc., Publisher 17

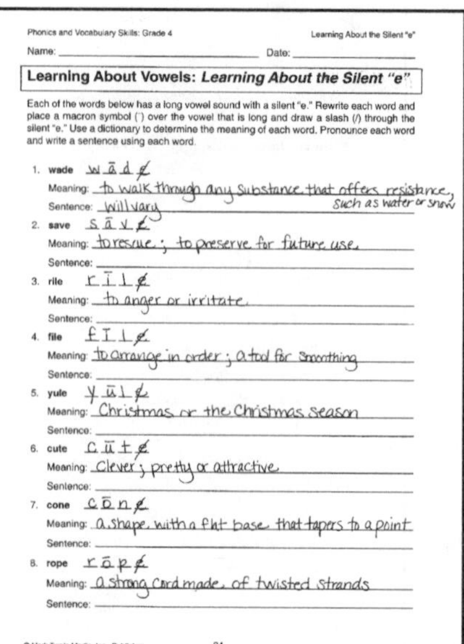

Phonics and Vocabulary Skills: Grade 4 Learning About the Silent "e"

Name: ______________________ Date: ______________

Learning About Vowels: ***Learning About the Silent "e"***

Some words follow the pattern "long vowel-consonant-silent e." In these words the final "e" is silent. For example, *like* is pronounced with a long "i" and silent "e."

Each of the following words has a short vowel sound. Place the letter "e" on the blank to make a word with a long vowel and a silent "e." Place the macron symbol (¯) over the long vowel and draw a slash through the silent "e." Use each new word in a sentence.

Example: not becomes nōte̸ *I wrote a note.*

1. bit becomes bīte̸
   Sentence: will vary
2. rat becomes rāte̸
   Sentence:
3. fat becomes fāte̸
   Sentence:
4. rod becomes rōde̸
   Sentence:
5. cut becomes cūte̸
   Sentence:
6. pin becomes pīne̸
   Sentence:
7. pan becomes pāne̸
   Sentence:
8. man becomes māne̸
   Sentence:

© Mark Twain Media, Inc., Publisher 18

Phonics and Vocabulary Skills: Grade 4 Learning About the Silent "e"

Name: ______________________ Date: ______________

Learning About Vowels: ***Learning About the Silent "e"***

Each of the words below has a long vowel sound with a silent "e." Rewrite each word and place a macron symbol (¯) over the vowel that is long and draw a slash (/) through the silent "e." Use a dictionary to determine the meaning of each word. Pronounce each word and write a sentence using each word.

1. **mile** m ī l e̸
   Meaning: a unit of linear measure equal to 5,280 feet
   Sentence: will vary
2. **rime** r ī m e̸
   Meaning: a word that corresponds to another in sound
   Sentence:
3. **rule** r ū l e̸
   Meaning: a regulation; an established practice that serves as a guide
   Sentence:
4. **home** h ō m e̸
   Meaning: the place where a person lives
   Sentence:
5. **mule** m ū l e̸
   Meaning: the offspring of a donkey and a horse
   Sentence:
6. **poke** p ō k e̸
   Meaning: to push or jab; a sack or bag
   Sentence:
7. **fate** f ā t e̸
   Meaning: destiny; something inevitable
   Sentence:
8. **wave** w ā v e̸
   Meaning: to move in a curving motion; a curve or undulation
   Sentence:

© Mark Twain Media, Inc., Publisher 19

Phonics and Vocabulary Skills: Grade 4 Learning About the Silent "e"

Name: ______________________ Date: ______________

Learning About Vowels: ***Learning About the Silent "e"***

Each of the words below has a long vowel sound with a silent "e." Rewrite each word and place a macron symbol (¯) over the vowel that is long and draw a slash (/) through the silent "e." Use a dictionary to determine the meaning of each word. Pronounce each word and write a sentence using each word.

1. **late** l ā t e̸
   Meaning: happening after the usual or expected time.
   Sentence: will vary
2. **safe** s ā f e̸
   Meaning: free from damage, danger, or injury; a locked container for valuables
   Sentence:
3. **role** r ō l e̸
   Meaning: a part an actor plays; a function or office assumed by someone
   Sentence:
4. **bile** b ī l e̸
   Meaning: bitter fluid secreted by the liver and stored in the gall bladder
   Sentence:
5. **bone** b ō n e̸
   Meaning: any of the parts of the skeleton of a vertebrate animal
   Sentence:
6. **lute** l ū t e̸
   Meaning: a stringed instrument related to the guitar
   Sentence:
7. **mete** m ē t e̸
   Meaning: to allot, distribute, apportion
   Sentence:
8. **pile** p ī l e̸
   Meaning: a mass of things heaped together
   Sentence:

© Mark Twain Media, Inc., Publisher 20

Phonics and Vocabulary Skills: Grade 4 Learning About the Silent "e"

Name: ______________________ Date: ______________

Learning About Vowels: ***Learning About the Silent "e"***

Each of the words below has a long vowel sound with a silent "e." Rewrite each word and place a macron symbol (¯) over the vowel that is long and draw a slash (/) through the silent "e." Use a dictionary to determine the meaning of each word. Pronounce each word and write a sentence using each word.

1. **wade** w ā d e̸
   Meaning: to walk through any substance that offers resistance, such as water or snow
   Sentence: will vary
2. **save** s ā v e̸
   Meaning: to rescue; to preserve for future use.
   Sentence:
3. **rile** r ī l e̸
   Meaning: to anger or irritate.
   Sentence:
4. **file** f ī l e̸
   Meaning: to arrange in order; a tool for smoothing
   Sentence:
5. **yule** y ū l e̸
   Meaning: Christmas or the Christmas season
   Sentence:
6. **cute** c ū t e̸
   Meaning: clever; pretty or attractive
   Sentence:
7. **cone** c ō n e̸
   Meaning: a shape with a flat base that tapers to a point
   Sentence:
8. **rope** r ō p e̸
   Meaning: a strong cord made of twisted strands
   Sentence:

© Mark Twain Media, Inc., Publisher 21

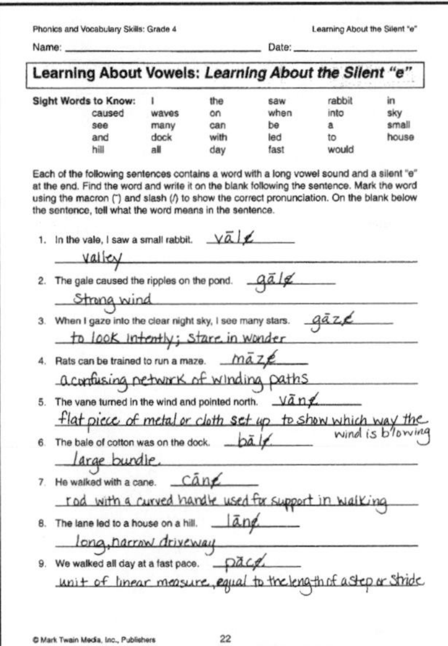

Phonics and Vocabulary Skills: Grade 4 — Learning About the Silent "e"

Name: ____________ Date: ____________

Learning About Vowels: *Learning About the Silent "e"*

Sight Words to Know: I, the, saw, rabbit, in, caused, waves, on, when, into, sky, see, many, can, be, a, small, and, dock, with, led, to, house, hill, all, day, fast, would

Each of the following sentences contains a word with a long vowel sound and a silent "e" at the end. Find the word and write it on the blank following the sentence. Mark the word using the macron (¯) and slash (/) to show the correct pronunciation. On the blank below the sentence, tell what the word means in the sentence.

1. In the vale, I saw a small rabbit. vāle̸
   valley
2. The gale caused the ripples on the pond. gāle̸
   Strong wind
3. When I gaze into the clear night sky, I see many stars. gāze̸
   to look intently; stare in wonder
4. Rats can be trained to run a maze. māze̸
   a confusing network of winding paths
5. The vane turned in the wind and pointed north. vāne̸
   flat piece of metal or cloth set up to show which way the wind is blowing
6. The bale of cotton was on the dock. bāle̸
   large bundle.
7. He walked with a cane. cāne̸
   rod with a curved handle used for support in walking
8. The lane led to a house on a hill. lāne̸
   long, narrow driveway
9. We walked all day at a fast pace. pāce̸
   unit of linear measure, equal to the length of a step or stride

© Mark Twain Media, Inc., Publishers 22

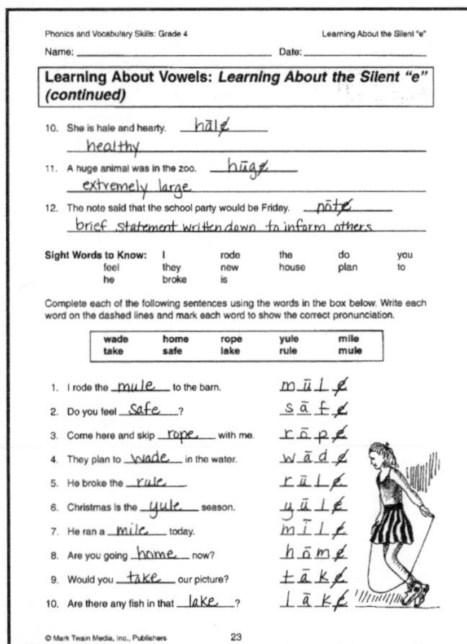

Phonics and Vocabulary Skills: Grade 4 — Learning About the Silent "e"

Name: ____________ Date: ____________

Learning About Vowels: *Learning About the Silent "e" (continued)*

10. She is hale and hearty. hāle̸
    healthy
11. A huge animal was in the zoo. hūge̸
    extremely large
12. The note said that the school party would be Friday. nōte̸
    brief statement written down to inform others

Sight Words to Know: I, rode, the, do, you, feel, they, new, house, plan, to, he, broke, is

Complete each of the following sentences using the words in the box below. Write each word on the dashed lines and mark each word to show the correct pronunciation.

wade	home	rope	yule	mile
take	safe	lake	rule	mule

1. I rode the mule to the barn. mūle̸
2. Do you feel safe? sāfe̸
3. Come here and skip rope with me. rōpe̸
4. They plan to wade in the water. wāde̸
5. He broke the rule. rūle̸
6. Christmas is the yule season. yūle̸
7. He ran a mile today. mīle̸
8. Are you going home now? hōme̸
9. Would you take our picture? tāke̸
10. Are there any fish in that lake? lāke̸

© Mark Twain Media, Inc., Publishers 23

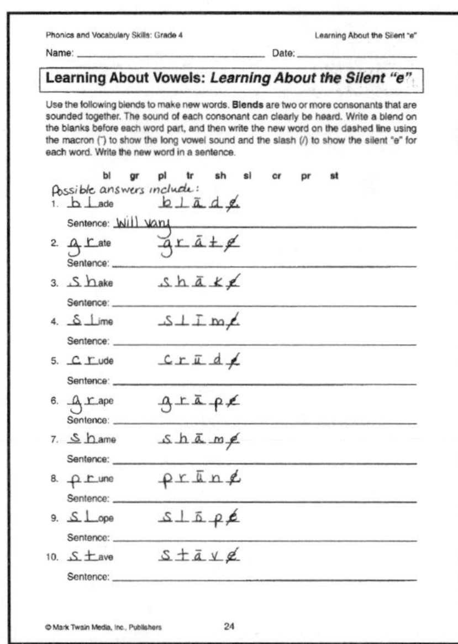

Phonics and Vocabulary Skills: Grade 4 — Learning About the Silent "e"

Name: ____________ Date: ____________

Learning About Vowels: *Learning About the Silent "e"*

Use the following blends to make new words. **Blends** are two or more consonants that are sounded together. The sound of each consonant can clearly be heard. Write a blend on the blanks before each word part, and then write the new word on the dashed line using the macron (¯) to show the long vowel sound and the slash (/) to show the silent "e" for each word. Write the new word in a sentence.

bl gr pl tr sh sl cr pr st

Possible answers include:

1. bl ade — blāde̸ — Sentence: Will vary
2. gr ate — grāte̸ — Sentence:
3. sh ake — shāke̸ — Sentence:
4. sl ime — slīme̸ — Sentence:
5. cr ude — crūde̸ — Sentence:
6. gr ape — grāpe̸ — Sentence:
7. sh ame — shāme̸ — Sentence:
8. pr une — prūne̸ — Sentence:
9. sl ope — slōpe̸ — Sentence:
10. st ave — stāve̸ — Sentence:

© Mark Twain Media, Inc., Publishers 24

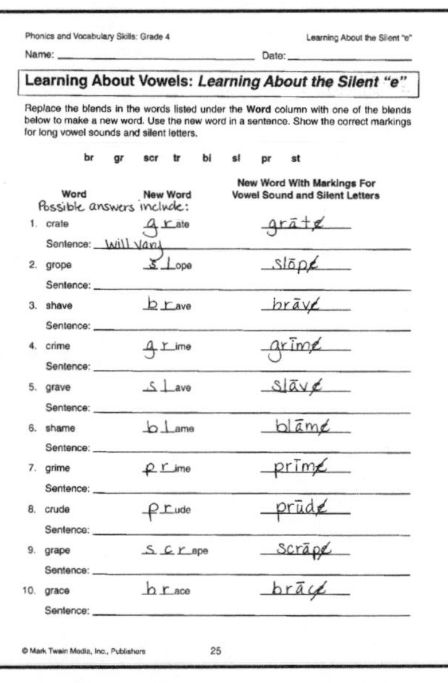

Phonics and Vocabulary Skills: Grade 4 — Learning About the Silent "e"

Name: ____________ Date: ____________

Learning About Vowels: *Learning About the Silent "e"*

Replace the blends in the words listed under the **Word** column with one of the blends below to make a new word. Use the new word in a sentence. Show the correct markings for long vowel sounds and silent letters.

br gr scr tr bl sl pr st

Possible answers include:

	Word	New Word	New Word With Markings For Vowel Sound and Silent Letters
1.	crate	gr ate	grāte̸
	Sentence: Will vary		
2.	grope	sl ope	slōpe̸
3.	shave	br ave	brāve̸
4.	crime	gr ime	grīme̸
5.	grave	sl ave	slāve̸
6.	shame	bl ame	blāme̸
7.	grime	pr ime	prīme̸
8.	crude	pr ude	prūde̸
9.	grape	scr ape	scrāpe̸
10.	grace	br ace	brāce̸

© Mark Twain Media, Inc., Publishers 25

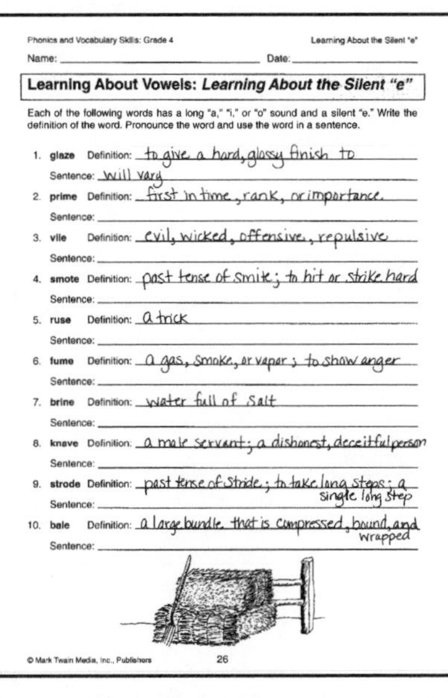

Phonics and Vocabulary Skills: Grade 4 — Learning About the Silent "e"

Name: ____________ Date: ____________

Learning About Vowels: *Learning About the Silent "e"*

Each of the following words has a long "a," "i," or "o" sound and a silent "e." Write the definition of the word. Pronounce the word and use the word in a sentence.

1. **glaze** Definition: to give a hard, glossy finish to — Sentence: will vary
2. **prime** Definition: first in time, rank, or importance. — Sentence:
3. **vile** Definition: evil, wicked, offensive, repulsive — Sentence:
4. **smote** Definition: past tense of smite; to hit or strike hard — Sentence:
5. **ruse** Definition: a trick — Sentence:
6. **fume** Definition: a gas, smoke, or vapor; to show anger — Sentence:
7. **brine** Definition: water full of salt — Sentence:
8. **knave** Definition: a male servant; a dishonest, deceitful person — Sentence:
9. **strode** Definition: past tense of stride; to take long steps; a single long step — Sentence:
10. **bale** Definition: a large bundle that is compressed, bound, and wrapped — Sentence:

© Mark Twain Media, Inc., Publishers 26

Phonics and Vocabulary Skills: Grade 4 — Reviewing What Has Been Learned

Name: ____________ Date: ____________

Learning About Vowels: Re*viewing What Has Been Learned*

Complete each of the following blanks.

1. Change the **s** in **sat** to **b** to make the word (a) bat. Make a sentence using the new word. (b) Sentences will vary
2. Change the **t** in **sat** to **d** to make the word (a) Sad. Make a sentence using the new word. (b) ____________
3. Change the **c** in **can** to **f** to make the word (a) fan. Make a sentence using the new word. (b) ____________
4. Change the **n** in **can** to **b** to make the word (a) cab. Make a sentence using the new word. (b) ____________
5. Add the letter **e** to **can** to make the word (a) cane. The vowel sound for **a** in **cane** is the (b) long sound and the vowel letter **e** is (c) silent. Make a sentence using the new word. (d) ____________

Change the blend to make a new word. Use the new word in a sentence.

1. Change the **br** in **bray** to **spr** to make the word spray. Sentence: will vary
2. Change the **pl** in **plate** to **sl** to make the word slate. Sentence:
3. Change the **dr** in **drab** to **cr** to make the word crab. Sentence:
4. Change the **fl** in **flare** to **gl** to make the word glare. Sentence:
5. Change the **sh** in **shame** to **fl** to make the word flame. Sentence:

© Mark Twain Media, Inc., Publishers 27

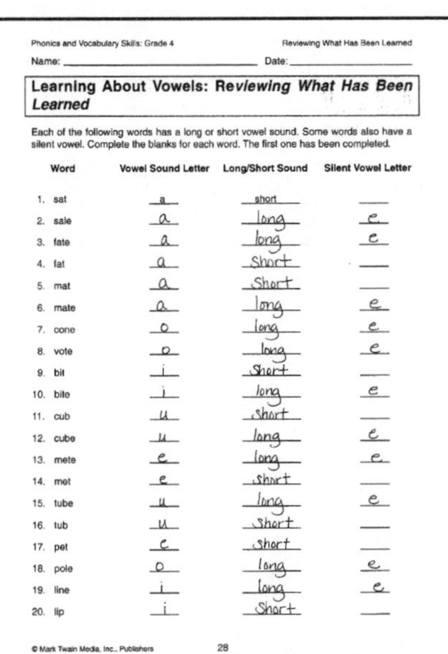

Phonics and Vocabulary Skills: Grade 4 — Reviewing What Has Been Learned

Name: ____________ Date: ____________

Learning About Vowels: Re*viewing What Has Been Learned*

Each of the following words has a long or short vowel sound. Some words also have a silent vowel. Complete the blanks for each word. The first one has been completed.

	Word	Vowel Sound Letter	Long/Short Sound	Silent Vowel Letter
1.	sat	a	short	
2.	sale	a	long	e
3.	fate	a	long	e
4.	fat	a	Short	
5.	mat	a	Short	
6.	mate	a	long	e
7.	cone	o	long	e
8.	vote	o	long	e
9.	bit	i	Short	
10.	bite	i	long	e
11.	cub	u	short	
12.	cube	u	long	e
13.	mete	e	long	e
14.	met	e	short	
15.	tube	u	long	e
16.	tub	u	Short	
17.	pet	e	short	
18.	pole	o	long	e
19.	line	i	long	e
20.	lip	i	Short	

© Mark Twain Media, Inc., Publishers 28

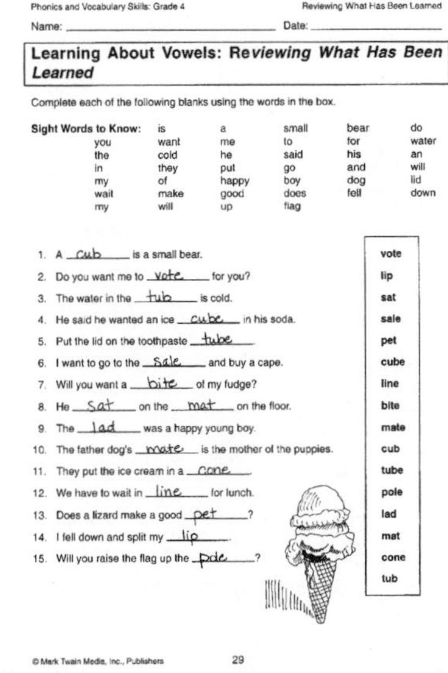

Phonics and Vocabulary Skills: Grade 4 — Reviewing What Has Been Learned

Name: ____________ Date: ____________

Learning About Vowels: Re*viewing What Has Been Learned*

Complete each of the following blanks using the words in the box.

Sight Words to Know: is, a, small, bear, do, you, want, me, to, for, water, the, cold, he, said, his, an, in, they, put, go, and, will, my, of, happy, boy, dog, lid, wait, make, good, does, fell, down, my, will, up, flag

Box: vote, lip, sat, sale, pet, cube, line, bite, mate, cub, tube, pole, lad, mat, cone, tub

1. A cub is a small bear.
2. Do you want me to vote for you?
3. The water in the tub is cold.
4. He said he wanted an ice cube in his soda.
5. Put the lid on the toothpaste tube.
6. I want to go to the sale and buy a cape.
7. Will you want a bite of my fudge?
8. He sat on the mat on the floor.
9. The lad was a happy young boy.
10. The father dog's mate is the mother of the puppies.
11. They put the ice cream in a cone.
12. We have to wait in line for lunch.
13. Does a lizard make a good pet?
14. I fell down and split my lip.
15. Will you raise the flag up the pole?

© Mark Twain Media, Inc., Publishers 29

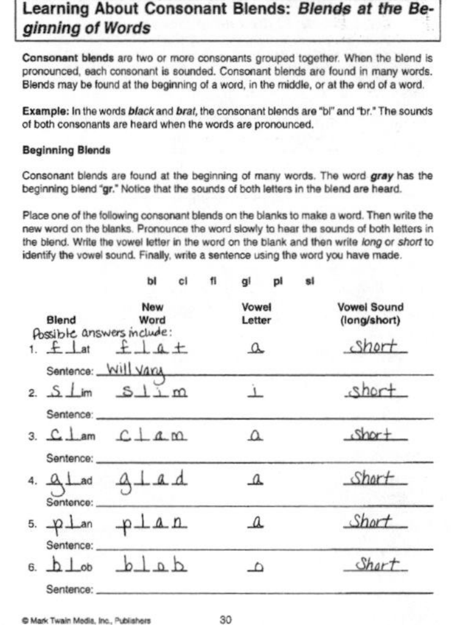

Phonics and Vocabulary Skills: Grade 4 — Blends at the Beginning of Words

Name: ____________ Date: ____________

Learning About Consonant Blends: *Blends at the Beginning of Words*

Consonant blends are two or more consonants grouped together. When the blend is pronounced, each consonant is sounded. Consonant blends are found in many words. Blends may be found at the beginning of a word, in the middle, or at the end of a word.

Example: In the words ***black*** and ***brat***, the consonant blends are "bl" and "br." The sounds of both consonants are heard when the words are pronounced.

Beginning Blends

Consonant blends are found at the beginning of many words. The word ***gray*** has the beginning blend "**gr.**" Notice that the sounds of both letters in the blend are heard.

Place one of the following consonant blends on the blanks to make a word. Then write the new word on the blanks. Pronounce the word slowly to hear the sounds of both letters in the blend. Write the vowel letter in the word on the blank and then write *long* or *short* to identify the vowel sound. Finally, write a sentence using the word you have made.

bl cl fl gl pl sl

Possible answers include:

	Blend	New Word	Vowel Letter	Vowel Sound (long/short)
1.	fl at	flat	a	Short
	Sentence: Will vary			
2.	sl im	slim	i	short
3.	cl am	clam	a	Short
4.	gl ad	glad	a	Short
5.	pl an	plan	a	Short
6.	bl ob	blob	o	Short

© Mark Twain Media, Inc., Publishers 30

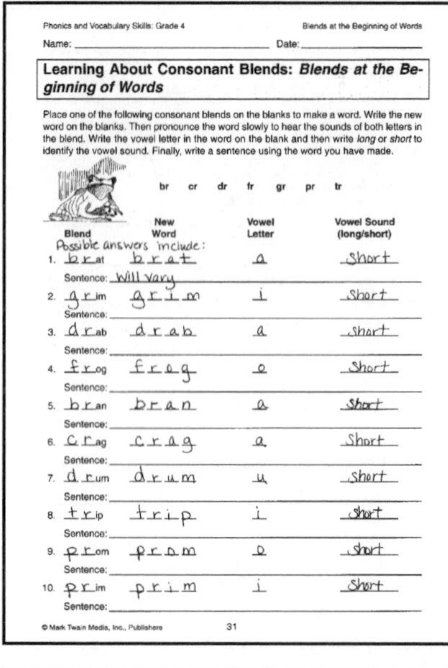

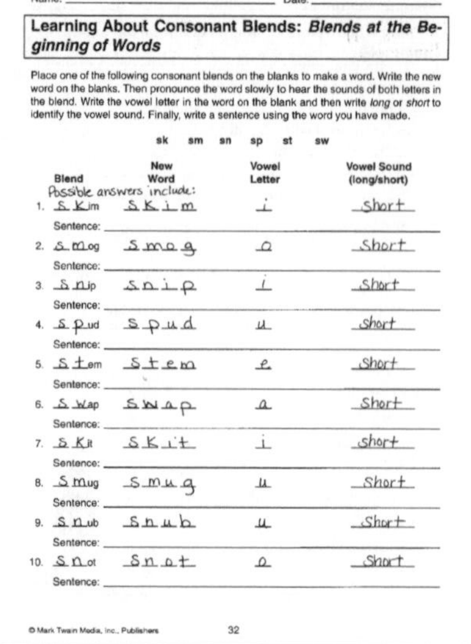

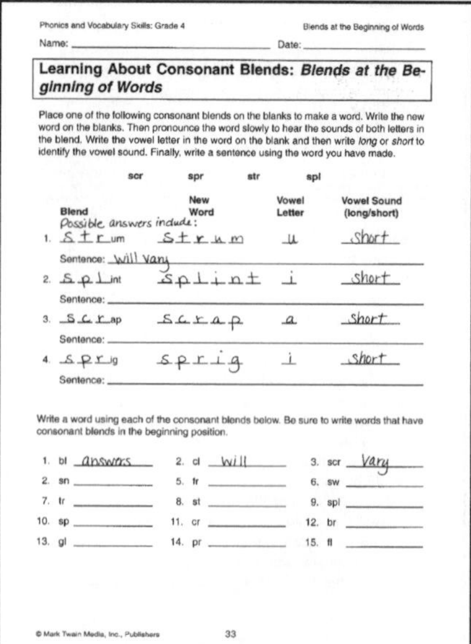

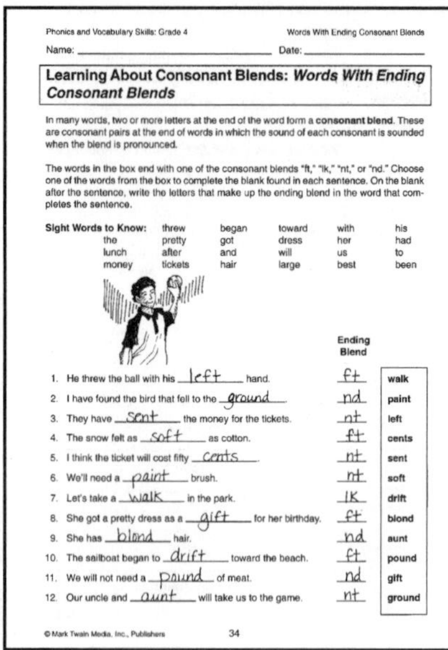

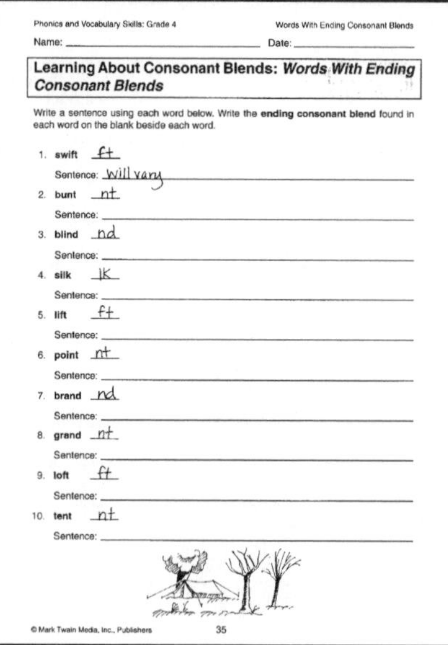

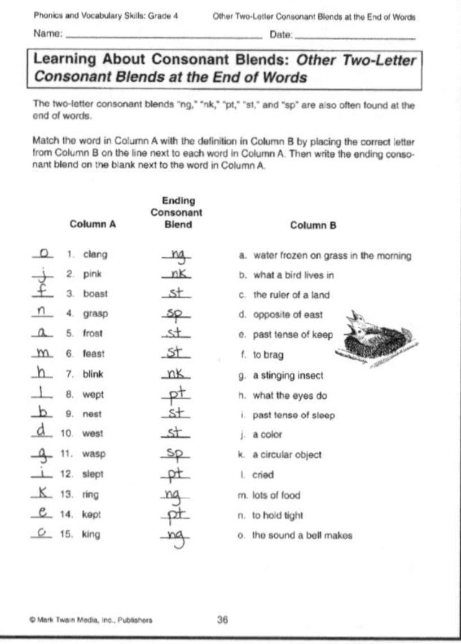

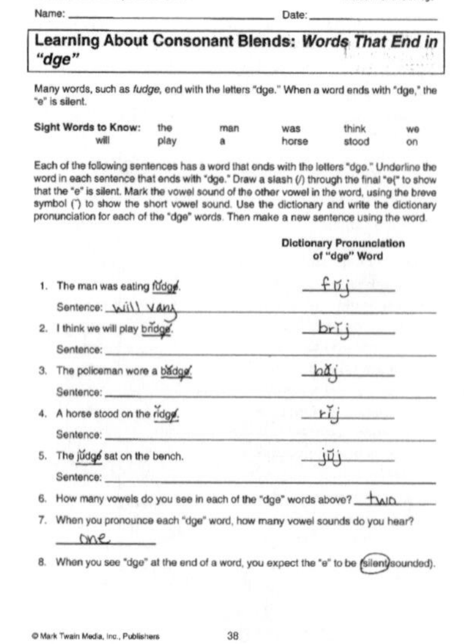

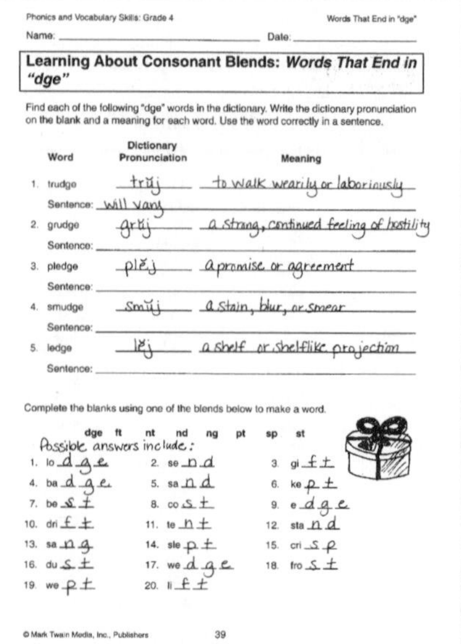

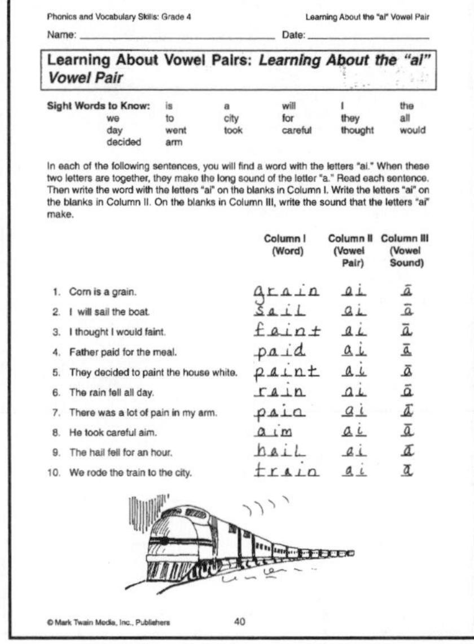

Phonics and Vocabulary Skills: Grade 4 Learning About the "ai" Vowel Pair

Name: ______ Date: ______

Learning About Vowel Pairs: *Learning About the "ai" Vowel Pair*

Sight Words to Know: is a will I the we to city for they all day went took careful thought would decided arm

In each of the following sentences, you will find a word with the letters "ai." When these two letters are together, they make the long sound of the letter "a." Read each sentence. Then write the word with the letters "ai" on the blanks in Column I. Write the letters "ai" on the blanks in Column II. On the blanks in Column III, write the sound that the letters "ai" make.

	Column I (Word)	Column II (Vowel Pair)	Column III (Vowel Sound)
1. Corn is a grain.	grain	ai	ā
2. I will sail the boat.	sail	ai	ā
3. I thought I would faint.	faint	ai	ā
4. Father paid for the meal.	paid	ai	ā
5. They decided to paint the house white.	paint	ai	ā
6. The rain fell all day.	rain	ai	ā
7. There was a lot of pain in my arm.	pain	ai	ā
8. He took careful aim.	aim	ai	ā
9. The hail fell for an hour.	hail	ai	ā
10. We rode the train to the city.	train	ai	ā

© Mark Twain Media, Inc., Publishers 40

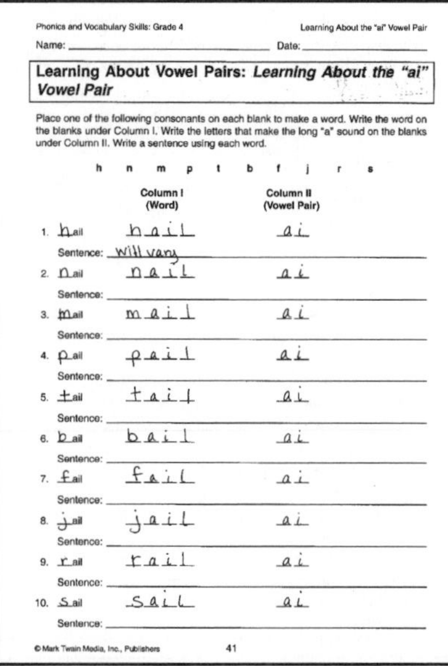

Phonics and Vocabulary Skills: Grade 4 Learning About the "ai" Vowel Pair

Name: ______ Date: ______

Learning About Vowel Pairs: *Learning About the "ai" Vowel Pair*

Place one of the following consonants on each blank to make a word. Write the word on the blanks under Column I. Write the letters that make the long "a" sound on the blanks under Column II. Write a sentence using each word.

h n m p t b f j r s

	Column I (Word)	Column II (Vowel Pair)
1. h ail	hail	ai
2. n ail	nail	ai
3. m ail	mail	ai
4. p ail	pail	ai
5. t ail	tail	ai
6. b ail	bail	ai
7. f ail	fail	ai
8. j ail	jail	ai
9. r ail	rail	ai
10. S ail	Sail	ai

Sentence: will vary

© Mark Twain Media, Inc., Publishers 41

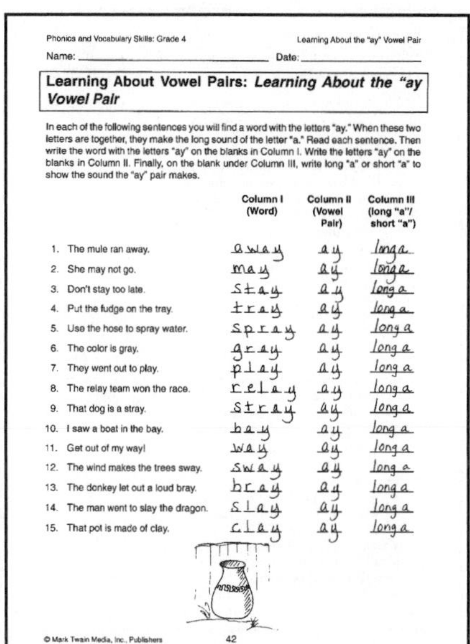

Phonics and Vocabulary Skills: Grade 4 Learning About the "ay" Vowel Pair

Name: ______ Date: ______

Learning About Vowel Pairs: *Learning About the "ay" Vowel Pair*

In each of the following sentences you will find a word with the letters "ay." When these two letters are together, they make the long sound of the letter "a." Read each sentence. Then write the word with the letters "ay" on the blanks in Column I. Write the letters "ay" on the blanks in Column II. Finally, on the blank under Column III, write long "a" or short "a" to show the sound the "ay" pair makes.

	Column I (Word)	Column II (Vowel Pair)	Column III (long "a"/ short "a")
1. The mule ran away.	away	ay	long a
2. She may not go.	may	ay	long a
3. Don't stay too late.	stay	ay	long a
4. Put the fudge on the tray.	tray	ay	long a
5. Use the hose to spray water.	spray	ay	long a
6. The color is gray.	gray	ay	long a
7. They went out to play.	play	ay	long a
8. The relay team won the race.	relay	ay	long a
9. That dog is a stray.	stray	ay	long a
10. I saw a boat in the bay.	bay	ay	long a
11. Get out of my way!	way	ay	long a
12. The wind makes the trees sway.	sway	ay	long a
13. The donkey let out a loud bray.	bray	ay	long a
14. The man went to slay the dragon.	slay	ay	long a
15. That pot is made of clay.	clay	ay	long a

© Mark Twain Media, Inc., Publishers 42

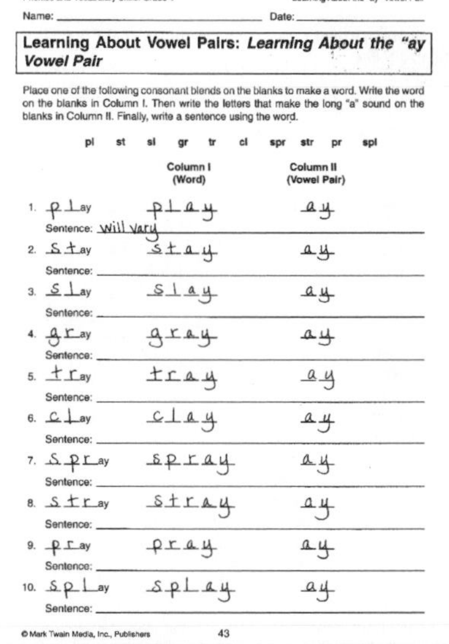

Phonics and Vocabulary Skills: Grade 4 Learning About the "ay" Vowel Pair

Name: ______ Date: ______

Learning About Vowel Pairs: *Learning About the "ay" Vowel Pair*

Place one of the following consonant blends on the blanks to make a word. Write the word on the blanks in Column I. Then write the letters that make the long "a" sound on the blanks in Column II. Finally, write a sentence using the word.

pl st sl gr tr cl spr str pr spl

	Column I (Word)	Column II (Vowel Pair)
1. pl ay	play	ay
2. St ay	stay	ay
3. Sl ay	slay	ay
4. gr ay	gray	ay
5. tr ay	tray	ay
6. cl ay	clay	ay
7. Spr ay	spray	ay
8. str ay	stray	ay
9. pr ay	pray	ay
10. Spl ay	splay	ay

Sentence: will vary

© Mark Twain Media, Inc., Publishers 43

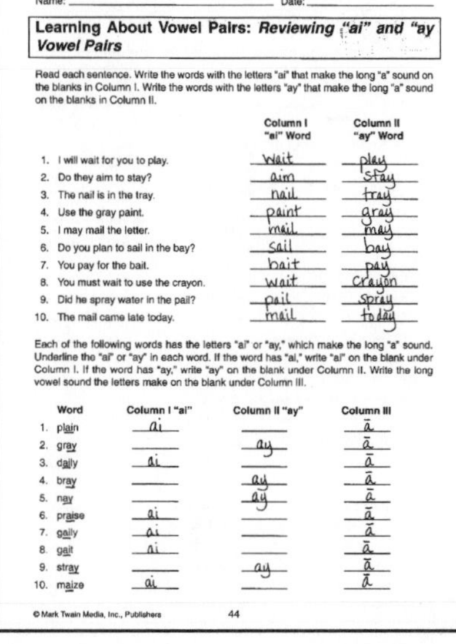

Phonics and Vocabulary Skills: Grade 4 Reviewing "ai" and "ay" Vowel Pairs

Name: ______ Date: ______

Learning About Vowel Pairs: *Reviewing "ai" and "ay" Vowel Pairs*

Read each sentence. Write the words with the letters "ai" that make the long "a" sound on the blanks in Column I. Write the words with the letters "ay" that make the long "a" sound on the blanks in Column II.

	Column I "ai" Word	Column II "ay" Word
1. I will wait for you to play.	wait	play
2. Do they aim to stay?	aim	stay
3. The nail is in the tray.	nail	tray
4. Use the gray paint.	paint	gray
5. I may mail the letter.	mail	may
6. Do you plan to sail in the bay?	sail	bay
7. You pay for the bait.	bait	pay
8. You must wait to use the crayon.	wait	crayon
9. Did he spray water in the pail?	pail	spray
10. The mail came late today.	mail	today

Each of the following words has the letters "ai" or "ay," which make the long "a" sound. Underline the "ai" or "ay" in each word. If the word has "ai," write "ai" on the blank under Column I. If the word has "ay," write "ay" on the blank under Column II. Write the long vowel sound the letters make on the blank under Column III.

Word	Column I "ai"	Column II "ay"	Column III
1. plain	ai		ā
2. gray		ay	ā
3. daily	ai		ā
4. bray		ay	ā
5. nay		ay	ā
6. praise	ai		ā
7. gaily	ai		ā
8. gait	ai		ā
9. stray		ay	ā
10. maize	ai		ā

© Mark Twain Media, Inc., Publishers 44

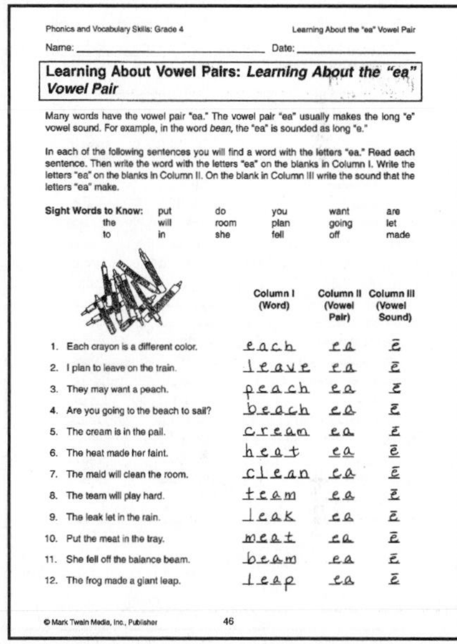

Phonics and Vocabulary Skills: Grade 4 Learning About the "ea" Vowel Pair

Name: ______ Date: ______

Learning About Vowel Pairs: *Learning About the "ea" Vowel Pair*

Many words have the vowel pair "ea." The vowel pair "ea" usually makes the long "e" vowel sound. For example, in the word *bean*, the "ea" is sounded as long "e."

In each of the following sentences you will find a word with the letters "ea." Read each sentence. Then write the word with the letters "ea" on the blanks in Column I. Write the letters "ea" on the blanks in Column II. On the blank in Column III write the sound that the letters "ea" make.

Sight Words to Know: put do you want are the will room plan going let to in she fell off made

	Column I (Word)	Column II (Vowel Pair)	Column III (Vowel Sound)
1. Each crayon is a different color.	each	ea	ē
2. I plan to leave on the train.	leave	ea	ē
3. They may want a peach.	peach	ea	ē
4. Are you going to the beach to sail?	beach	ea	ē
5. The cream is in the pail.	cream	ea	ē
6. The heat made her faint.	heat	ea	ē
7. The maid will clean the room.	clean	ea	ē
8. The team will play hard.	team	ea	ē
9. The leak let in the rain.	leak	ea	ē
10. Put the meat in the tray.	meat	ea	ē
11. She fell off the balance beam.	beam	ea	ē
12. The frog made a giant leap.	leap	ea	ē

© Mark Twain Media, Inc., Publisher 46

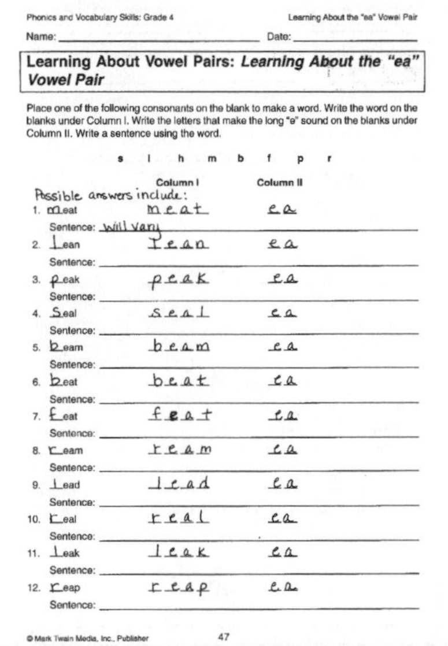

Phonics and Vocabulary Skills: Grade 4 Learning About the "ea" Vowel Pair

Name: ______ Date: ______

Learning About Vowel Pairs: *Learning About the "ea" Vowel Pair*

Place one of the following consonants on the blank to make a word. Write the word on the blanks under Column I. Write the letters that make the long "e" sound on the blanks under Column II. Write a sentence using the word.

s l h m b f p r

Possible answers include:

	Column I	Column II
1. m eat	meat	ea
2. l ean	lean	ea
3. p eak	peak	ea
4. S eal	seal	ea
5. b eam	beam	ea
6. b eat	beat	ea
7. f eat	feat	ea
8. r eam	ream	ea
9. l ead	lead	ea
10. r eal	real	ea
11. l eak	leak	ea
12. r eap	reap	ea

Sentence: will vary

© Mark Twain Media, Inc., Publisher 47

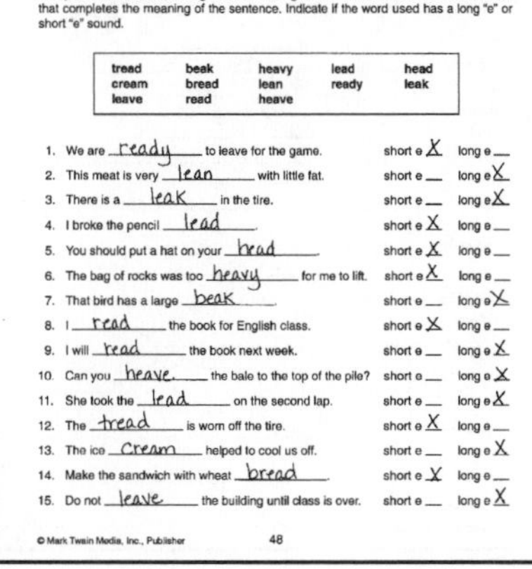

Phonics and Vocabulary Skills: Grade 4 Other "ea" Sounds

Name: ______ Date: ______

Learning About Vowel Pairs: *Other "ea" Sounds*

You have learned that when a word has the "ea" vowel pair, the long "e" sound is often heard. However, there are many words with "ea" that are pronounced with the short "e" sound. The way the word is used in a sentence often gives a clue to the pronunciation of "ea" words.

Example: "ea" word with long "e" sound = read = I will read the paper tomorrow. "ea" word with short "e" sound = read = I read the paper yesterday.

Complete each of the following sentences using one of the words below. Choose a word that completes the meaning of the sentence. Indicate if the word used has a long "e" or short "e" sound.

tread	beak	heavy	lead	head
cream	bread	lean	ready	leak
leave	read	heave		

	short e	long e
1. We are ready to leave for the game.	X	
2. This meat is very lean with little fat.		X
3. There is a leak in the tire.		X
4. I broke the pencil lead.	X	
5. You should put a hat on your head.	X	
6. The bag of rocks was too heavy for me to lift.	X	
7. That bird has a large beak.		X
8. I read the book for English class.	X	
9. I will read the book next week.		X
10. Can you heave the bale to the top of the pile?		X
11. She took the lead on the second lap.		X
12. The tread is worn off the tire.	X	
13. The ice cream helped to cool us off.		X
14. Make the sandwich with wheat bread.	X	
15. Do not leave the building until class is over.		X

© Mark Twain Media, Inc., Publisher 48

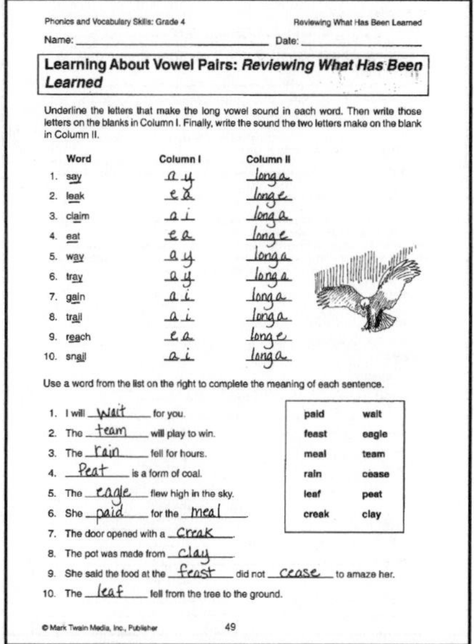

Phonics and Vocabulary Skills: Grade 4 Reviewing What Has Been Learned

Name: ______ Date: ______

Learning About Vowel Pairs: *Reviewing What Has Been Learned*

Underline the letters that make the long vowel sound in each word. Then write those letters on the blanks in Column I. Finally, write the sound the two letters make on the blank in Column II.

Word	Column I	Column II
1. say	ay	long a
2. leak	ea	long e
3. claim	ai	long a
4. eat	ea	long e
5. way	ay	long a
6. tray	ay	long a
7. gain	ai	long a
8. trail	ai	long a
9. reach	ea	long e
10. snail	ai	long a

Use a word from the list on the right to complete the meaning of each sentence.

1. I will wait for you.
2. The team will play to win.
3. The rain fell for hours.
4. Peat is a form of coal.
5. The eagle flew high in the sky.
6. She paid for the meal
7. The door opened with a creak
8. The pot was made from clay
9. She said the food at the feast did not cease to amaze her.
10. The leaf fell from the tree to the ground.

paid	wait
feast	eagle
meal	team
rain	cease
leaf	peat
creak	clay

© Mark Twain Media, Inc., Publisher 49

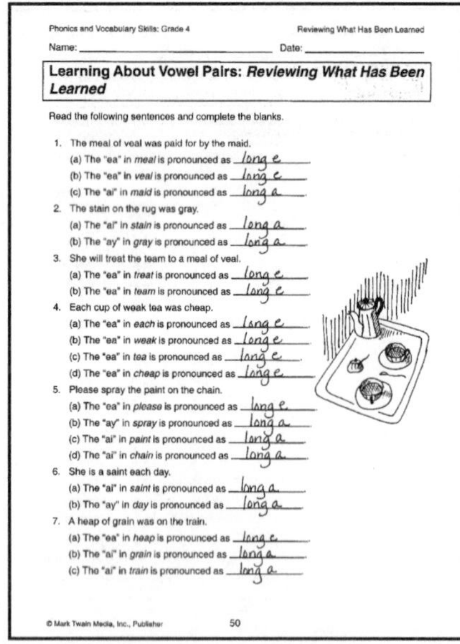

Phonics and Vocabulary Skills: Grade 4 Reviewing What Has Been Learned

Name: ______ Date: ______

Learning About Vowel Pairs: *Reviewing What Has Been Learned*

Read the following sentences and complete the blanks.

1. The meal of veal was paid for by the maid.
   (a) The "ea" in *meal* is pronounced as long e
   (b) The "ea" in *veal* is pronounced as long e
   (c) The "ai" in *maid* is pronounced as long a
2. The stain on the rug was gray.
   (a) The "ai" in *stain* is pronounced as long a
   (b) The "ay" in *gray* is pronounced as long a
3. She will treat the team to a meal of veal.
   (a) The "ea" in *treat* is pronounced as long e
   (b) The "ea" in *team* is pronounced as long e
4. Each cup of weak tea was cheap.
   (a) The "ea" in *each* is pronounced as long e
   (b) The "ea" in *weak* is pronounced as long e
   (c) The "ea" in *tea* is pronounced as long e
   (d) The "ea" in *cheap* is pronounced as long e
5. Please spray the paint on the chain.
   (a) The "ea" in *please* is pronounced as long e
   (b) The "ay" in *spray* is pronounced as long a
   (c) The "ai" in *paint* is pronounced as long a
   (d) The "ai" in *chain* is pronounced as long a
6. She is a saint each day.
   (a) The "ai" in *saint* is pronounced as long a
   (b) The "ay" in *day* is pronounced as long a
7. A heap of grain was on the train.
   (a) The "ea" in *heap* is pronounced as long e
   (b) The "ai" in *grain* is pronounced as long a
   (c) The "ai" in *train* is pronounced as long a

© Mark Twain Media, Inc., Publisher 50

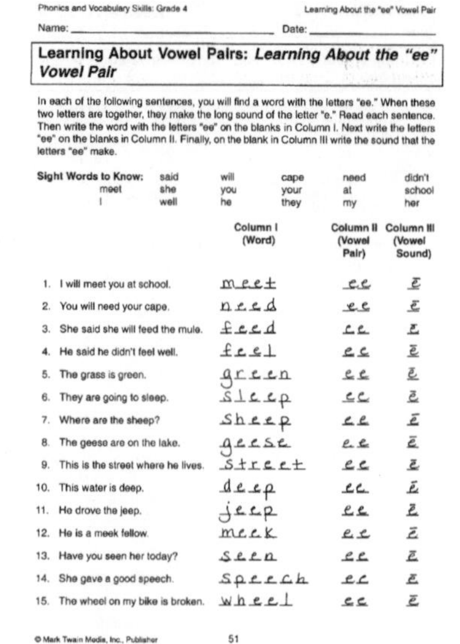

Phonics and Vocabulary Skills: Grade 4 Learning About the "ee" Vowel Pair

Name: ______ Date: ______

Learning About Vowel Pairs: *Learning About the "ee" Vowel Pair*

In each of the following sentences, you will find a word with the letters "ee." When these two letters are together, they make the long sound of the letter "e." Read each sentence. Then write the word with the letters "ee" on the blanks in Column I. Next write the letters "ee" on the blanks in Column II. Finally, on the blank in Column III write the sound that the letters "ee" make.

Sight Words to Know: said, will, cape, need, didn't, meet, she, you, your, at, school, I, well, he, they, my, her

	Column I (Word)	Column II (Vowel Pair)	Column III (Vowel Sound)
1. I will meet you at school.	meet	ee	ē
2. You will need your cape.	need	ee	ē
3. She said she will feed the mule.	feed	ee	ē
4. He said he didn't feel well.	feel	ee	ē
5. The grass is green.	green	ee	ē
6. They are going to sleep.	sleep	ee	ē
7. Where are the sheep?	sheep	ee	ē
8. The geese are on the lake.	geese	ee	ē
9. This is the street where he lives.	street	ee	ē
10. This water is deep.	deep	ee	ē
11. He drove the jeep.	jeep	ee	ē
12. He is a meek fellow.	meek	ee	ē
13. Have you seen her today?	seen	ee	ē
14. She gave a good speech.	speech	ee	ē
15. The wheel on my bike is broken.	wheel	ee	ē

© Mark Twain Media, Inc., Publisher 51

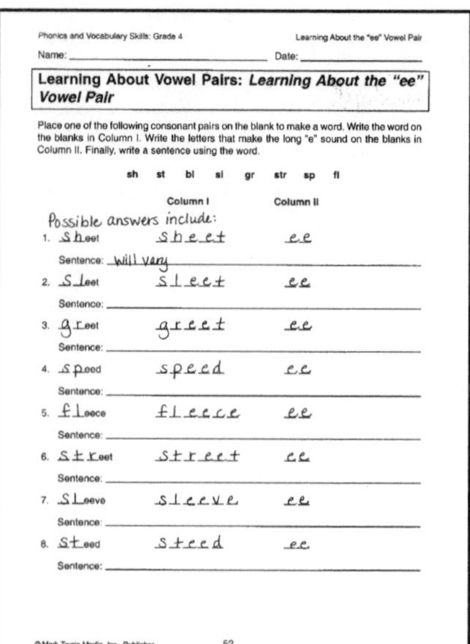

Phonics and Vocabulary Skills: Grade 4 Learning About the "ee" Vowel Pair

Name: ______ Date: ______

Learning About Vowel Pairs: *Learning About the "ee" Vowel Pair*

Place one of the following consonant pairs on the blank to make a word. Write the word on the blanks in Column I. Write the letters that make the long "e" sound on the blanks in Column II. Finally, write a sentence using the word.

sh st bl sl gr str sp fl

Possible answers include:

	Column I	Column II
1. sh eet	sheet	ee
2. sl eet	sleet	ee
3. gr eet	greet	ee
4. sp eed	speed	ee
5. fl eece	fleece	ee
6. str eet	street	ee
7. sl eeve	sleeve	ee
8. st eed	steed	ee

Sentence: will vary

© Mark Twain Media, Inc., Publisher 52

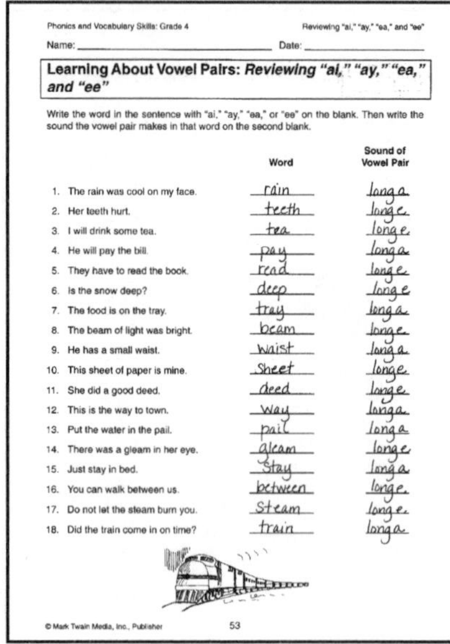

Phonics and Vocabulary Skills: Grade 4 Reviewing "ai," "ay," "ea," and "ee"

Name: ______ Date: ______

Learning About Vowel Pairs: *Reviewing "ai," "ay," "ea," and "ee"*

Write the word in the sentence with "ai," "ay," "ea," or "ee" on the blank. Then write the sound the vowel pair makes in that word on the second blank.

	Word	Sound of Vowel Pair
1. The rain was cool on my face.	rain	long a
2. Her teeth hurt.	teeth	long e
3. I will drink some tea.	tea	long e
4. He will pay the bill.	pay	long a
5. They have to read the book.	read	long e
6. Is the snow deep?	deep	long e
7. The food is on the tray.	tray	long a
8. The beam of light was bright.	beam	long e
9. He has a small waist.	waist	long a
10. This sheet of paper is mine.	sheet	long e
11. She did a good deed.	deed	long e
12. This is the way to town.	way	long a
13. Put the water in the pail.	pail	long a
14. There was a gleam in her eye.	gleam	long e
15. Just stay in bed.	stay	long a
16. You can walk between us.	between	long e
17. Do not let the steam burn you.	steam	long e
18. Did the train come in on time?	train	long a

© Mark Twain Media, Inc., Publisher 53

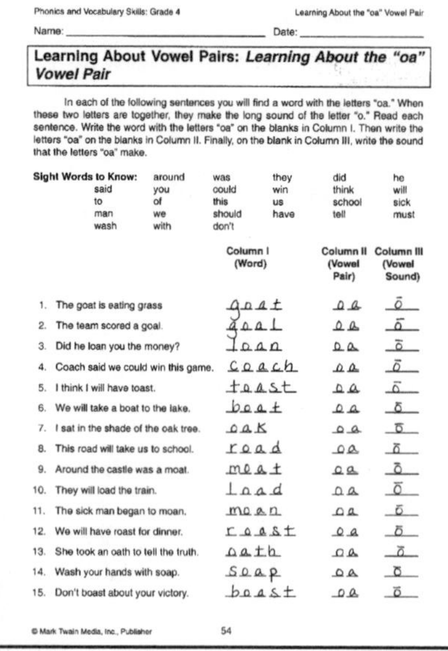

Phonics and Vocabulary Skills: Grade 4 Learning About the "oa" Vowel Pair

Name: ______ Date: ______

Learning About Vowel Pairs: *Learning About the "oa" Vowel Pair*

In each of the following sentences you will find a word with the letters "oa." When these two letters are together, they make the long sound of the letter "o." Read each sentence. Write the word with the letters "oa" on the blanks in Column I. Then write the letters "oa" on the blanks in Column II. Finally, on the blank in Column III, write the sound that the letters "oa" make.

Sight Words to Know: around, was, they, did, he, said, you, could, win, think, will, to, of, this, us, school, sick, man, we, should, have, tell, must, wash, with, don't

	Column I (Word)	Column II (Vowel Pair)	Column III (Vowel Sound)
1. The goat is eating grass	goat	oa	ō
2. The team scored a goal.	goal	oa	ō
3. Did he loan you the money?	loan	oa	ō
4. Coach said we could win this game.	coach	oa	ō
5. I think I will have toast.	toast	oa	ō
6. We will take a boat to the lake.	boat	oa	ō
7. I sat in the shade of the oak tree.	oak	oa	ō
8. This road will take us to school.	road	oa	ō
9. Around the castle was a moat.	moat	oa	ō
10. They will load the train.	load	oa	ō
11. The sick man began to moan.	moan	oa	ō
12. We will have roast for dinner.	roast	oa	ō
13. She took an oath to tell the truth.	oath	oa	ō
14. Wash your hands with soap.	soap	oa	ō
15. Don't boast about your victory.	boast	oa	ō

© Mark Twain Media, Inc., Publisher 54

Phonics and Vocabulary Skills: Grade 4 Learning About the "oa" Vowel Pair

Name: ______ Date: ______

Learning About Vowel Pairs: *Learning About the "oa" Vowel Pair*

Place the following consonants on the blanks to make a word. Write the word on the blanks in Column I. Then write the letters that make the long "o" sound on the blanks in Column II. Finally, write a sentence using the word.

thr c l t gl cl fl r

Possible answers include:

	Column I	Column II
1. gl oat	gloat	oa
2. fl oat	float	oa
3. c oal	coal	oa
4. l oaf	loaf	oa
5. r oam	roam	oa
6. c oach	coach	oa
7. t oast	toast	oa
8. thr oat	throat	oa
9. cl oak	cloak	oa
10. r oast	roast	oa

Sentence: will vary

© Mark Twain Media, Inc., Publisher 55

Phonics and Vocabulary Skills: Grade 4 Learning About the "ei" Vowel Pair

Name: ______ Date: ______

Learning About Vowel Pairs: *Learning About the "ei" Vowel Pair*

In many words that have a vowel combination, the first vowel is given the long sound and the second vowel is silent. However, there are other times when the sound of the vowel combination will depend on the word in which it is found. The best way to determine the sound of these vowel combinations is to determine how the word should be pronounced so that it makes sense in a sentence.

The vowel pair "ei" is found in many words. In the words below, the vowels "ei" will have the the long "e" sound as in *either* or the long "a" sound as in *eight*.

Example: **ei**ther = long "e" sound Example: **ei**ght = long "a" sound

In each of the following words, the "ei" vowels have the long sound of "e" or the long sound of "a." Place each of the following words on the correct blank to show the sound of "ei." The first two have been completed for you. On the blank below each word, write a sentence using the word. **Hint:** If you do not know how to pronounce a word, try both the long "e" and long "a" sounds to see if either sound gives a word you know.

Word	Long "e"	Long "a"
1. either	*either*	
2. eight		*eight*
3. ceiling	ceiling	
4. rein		rein
5. freight		freight
6. weight		weight
7. neither	neither	
8. neighbor		neighbor

Sentence: will vary

© Mark Twain Media, Inc., Publisher 56

Phonics and Vocabulary Skills: Grade 4 Learning About the "ie" Vowel Pair

Name: ______ Date: ______

Learning About Vowel Pairs: *Learning About the "ie" Vowel Pair*

In each of the following words, the "ie" vowelpair has either the long "i" sound or the long "e" sound. The long sound of "i" is found in the word *die*. The long sound of "e" is found in the word *field*. Place each of the following words on the correct blank to show the sound "ie" makes. The first two have been completed for you. On the blank below each word, write a sentence using the word. **Hint:** If you do not know how to pronounce a word, try both the long "i" and long "e" sounds. See which sound gives a word you know.

Word	Long "i"	Long "e"
1. pie	*pie*	
2. field		*field*
3. cried	cried	
4. fried	fried	
5. chief		chief
6. piece		piece
7. tried	tried	
8. relief		relief
9. dried	dried	
10. shield		shield

Sentence: will vary

© Mark Twain Media, Inc., Publisher 57

Phonics and Vocabulary Skills: Grade 4 Learning About the "ey" Vowel Pair

Name: ______ Date: ______

Learning About Vowel Pairs: *Learning About the "ey" Vowel Pair*

In some words, the letter combination "ey" has a long "e" sound. In other words, the "ey" combination makes the long "a" sound.

Example: donk**ey** = long "e" sound **Example:** h**ey** = long "a" sound

Read each of the following sentences and place one of the words from the box below on the blank. Then circle whether that word has a long "e" sound or a long "a" sound. **Hint:** If a word does not make sense using one long sound, try the other long sound.

Sight Words to Know: try, to, find, where, the, have, how, much, do, you, they, with, of, think, must, are, saw, him, that, birds, flew, don't, walk, dark

money	honey	obey	covey	prey	hockey
they	alley	convey	key	barley	kidney

Sentence	Circled
1. Open the door with your key.	long "e"
2. How much money do you have with you?	long "e"
3. They plan to play a game of hockey.	long "e"
4. Do you think they will be on time?	long "a"
5. We must obey the rules.	long "a"
6. They are having kidney beans for lunch.	long "e"
7. Barley is a grain similar to wheat.	long "e"
8. Eagles prey on mice.	long "a"
9. Please convey the message that I will be late.	long "a"
10. Honey is a sweet substance made by bees.	long "e"

HONEY

© Mark Twain Media, Inc., Publisher 58

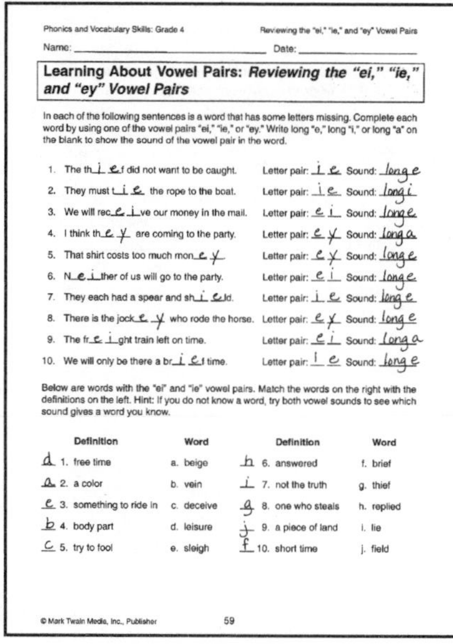
Phonics and Vocabulary Skills: Grade 4 — Reviewing the "ei," "ie," and "ey" Vowel Pairs

Name: Date:

Learning About Vowel Pairs: *Reviewing the "ei," "ie," and "ey" Vowel Pairs*

In each of the following sentences is a word that has some letters missing. Complete each word by using one of the vowel pairs "ei," "ie," or "ey." Write long "e," long "i," or long "a" on the blank to show the sound of the vowel pair in the word.

1. The thief did not want to be caught. Letter pair: ie Sound: long e
2. They must tie the rope to the boat. Letter pair: ie Sound: long i
3. We will receive our money in the mail. Letter pair: ei Sound: long e
4. I think they are coming to the party. Letter pair: ey Sound: long a
5. That shirt costs too much money. Letter pair: ey Sound: long e
6. Neither of us will go to the party. Letter pair: ei Sound: long e
7. They each had a spear and shield. Letter pair: ie Sound: long e
8. There is the jockey who rode the horse. Letter pair: ey Sound: long e
9. The freight train left on time. Letter pair: ei Sound: long a
10. We will only be there a brief time. Letter pair: ie Sound: long e

Below are words with the "ei" and "ie" vowel pairs. Match the words on the right with the definitions on the left. Hint: If you do not know a word, try both vowel sounds to see which sound gives a word you know.

Definition	Word	Definition	Word
d 1. free time	a. beige	h 6. answered	f. brief
a 2. a color	b. vein	i 7. not the truth	g. thief
e 3. something to ride in	c. deceive	g 8. one who steals	h. replied
b 4. body part	d. leisure	j 9. a piece of land	i. lie
c 5. try to fool	e. sleigh	f 10. short time	j. field

© Mark Twain Media, Inc., Publisher 59

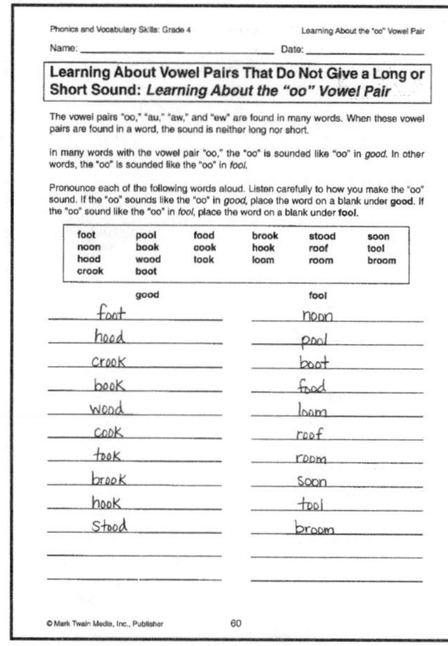
Phonics and Vocabulary Skills: Grade 4 — Learning About the "oo" Vowel Pair

Name: Date:

Learning About Vowel Pairs That Do Not Give a Long or Short Sound: *Learning About the "oo" Vowel Pair*

The vowel pairs "oo," "au," "aw," and "ew" are found in many words. When these vowel pairs are found in a word, the sound is neither long nor short.

In many words with the vowel pair "oo," the "oo" is sounded like "oo" in *good*. In other words, the "oo" is sounded like the "oo" in *fool*.

Pronounce each of the following words aloud. Listen carefully to how you make the "oo" sound. If the "oo" sounds like the "oo" in *good*, place the word on a blank under **good**. If the "oo" sound like the "oo" in *fool*, place the word on a blank under **fool**.

foot	pool	food	brook	stood	soon
noon	book	cook	hook	roof	tool
hood	wood	took	loom	room	broom
crook	boot				

good	fool
foot	noon
hood	pool
crook	boot
book	food
wood	loom
cook	roof
took	room
brook	soon
hook	tool
stood	broom

© Mark Twain Media, Inc., Publisher 60

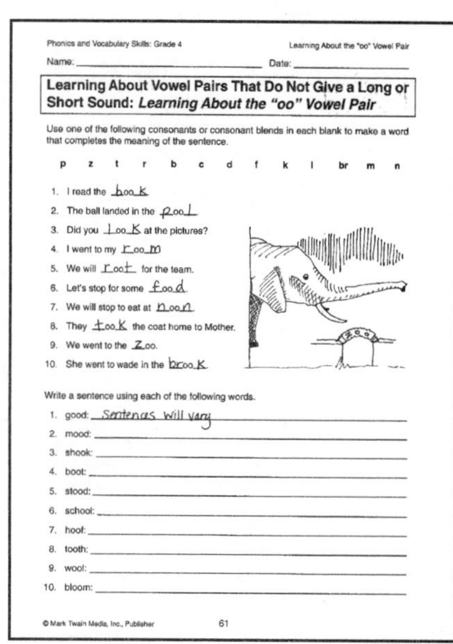
Phonics and Vocabulary Skills: Grade 4 — Learning About the "oo" Vowel Pair

Name: Date:

Learning About Vowel Pairs That Do Not Give a Long or Short Sound: *Learning About the "oo" Vowel Pair*

Use one of the following consonants or consonant blends in each blank to make a word that completes the meaning of the sentence.

p z t r b c d f k l br m n

1. I read the book.
2. The ball landed in the pool.
3. Did you look at the pictures?
4. I went to my room.
5. We will root for the team.
6. Let's stop for some food.
7. We will stop to eat at noon.
8. They took the coat home to Mother.
9. We went to the zoo.
10. She went to wade in the brook.

Write a sentence using each of the following words.

1. good: Sentences will vary
2. mood:
3. shook:
4. boot:
5. stood:
6. school:
7. hoof:
8. tooth:
9. wool:
10. bloom:

© Mark Twain Media, Inc., Publisher 61

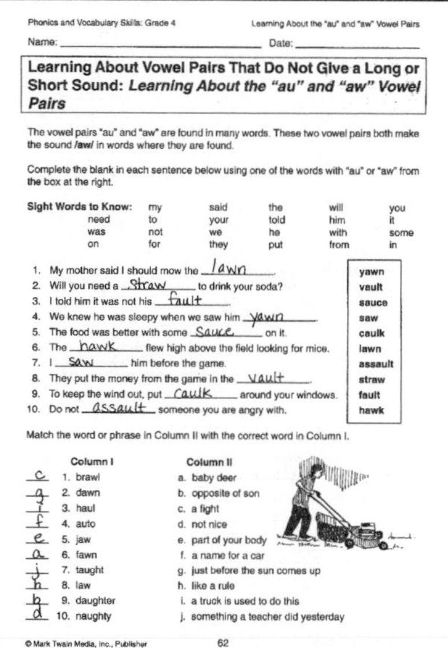
Phonics and Vocabulary Skills: Grade 4 — Learning About the "au" and "aw" Vowel Pairs

Name: Date:

Learning About Vowel Pairs That Do Not Give a Long or Short Sound: *Learning About the "au" and "aw" Vowel Pairs*

The vowel pairs "au" and "aw" are found in many words. These two vowel pairs both make the sound /aw/ in words where they are found.

Complete the blank in each sentence below using one of the words with "au" or "aw" from the box at the right.

Sight Words to Know: my, said, the, will, you, need, to, your, told, him, it, was, not, we, he, with, some, on, for, they, put, from, in

1. My mother said I should mow the lawn.
2. Will you need a straw to drink your soda?
3. I told him it was not his fault.
4. We knew he was sleepy when we saw him yawn.
5. The food was better with some sauce on it.
6. The hawk flew high above the field looking for mice.
7. I saw him before the game.
8. They put the money from the game in the vault.
9. To keep the wind out, put caulk around your windows.
10. Do not assault someone you are angry with.

yawn, vault, sauce, saw, caulk, lawn, assault, straw, fault, hawk

Match the word or phrase in Column II with the correct word in Column I.

Column I	Column II
c 1. brawl	a. baby deer
g 2. dawn	b. opposite of son
i 3. haul	c. a fight
f 4. auto	d. not nice
e 5. jaw	e. part of your body
a 6. fawn	f. a name for a car
j 7. taught	g. just before the sun comes up
h 8. law	h. like a rule
b 9. daughter	i. a truck is used to do this
d 10. naughty	j. something a teacher did yesterday

© Mark Twain Media, Inc., Publisher 62

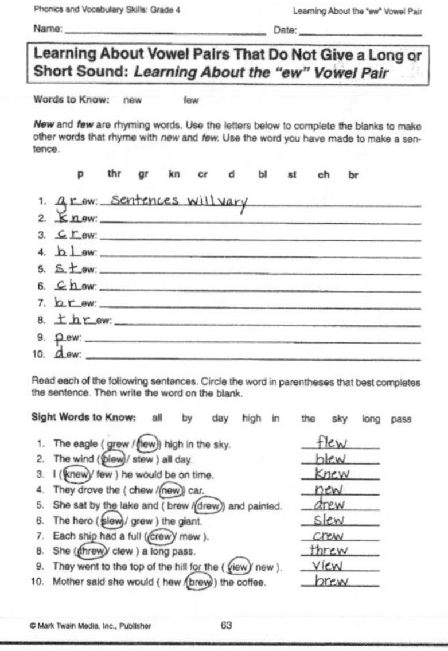
Phonics and Vocabulary Skills: Grade 4 — Learning About the "ew" Vowel Pair

Name: Date:

Learning About Vowel Pairs That Do Not Give a Long or Short Sound: *Learning About the "ew" Vowel Pair*

Words to Know: new few

New and *few* are rhyming words. Use the letters below to complete the blanks to make other words that rhyme with *new* and *few*. Use the word you have made to make a sentence.

p thr gr kn cr d bl st ch br

1. grew: Sentences will vary
2. knew:
3. crew:
4. blew:
5. stew:
6. chew:
7. brew:
8. threw:
9. pew:
10. dew:

Read each of the following sentences. Circle the word in parentheses that best completes the sentence. Then write the word on the blank.

Sight Words to Know: all by day high in the sky long pass

1. The eagle (grew / flew) high in the sky. flew
2. The wind (blew / stew) all day. blew
3. I (knew / few) he would be on time. knew
4. They drove the (chew / new) car. new
5. She sat by the lake and (brew / drew) and painted. drew
6. The hero (slew / grew) the giant. slew
7. Each ship had a full (crew / mew). crew
8. She (threw / clew) a long pass. threw
9. They went to the top of the hill for the (view / new). view
10. Mother said she would (hew / brew) the coffee. brew

© Mark Twain Media, Inc., Publisher 63

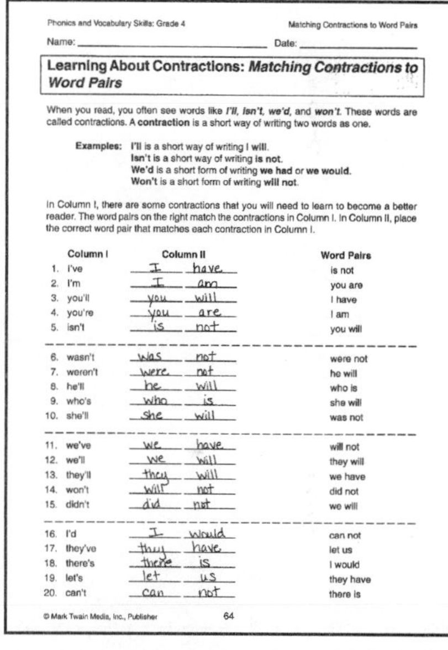
Phonics and Vocabulary Skills: Grade 4 — Matching Contractions to Word Pairs

Name: Date:

Learning About Contractions: *Matching Contractions to Word Pairs*

When you read, you often see words like *I'll, isn't, we'd,* and *won't*. These words are called contractions. A **contraction** is a short way of writing two words as one.

Examples: **I'll** is a short way of writing **I will**. **Isn't** is a short way of writing **is not**. **We'd** is a short form of writing **we had** or **we would**. **Won't** is a short form of writing **will not**.

In Column I, there are some contractions that you will need to learn to become a better reader. The word pairs on the right match the contractions in Column I. In Column II, place the correct word pair that matches each contraction in Column I.

Column I	Column II	Word Pairs
1. I've	I have	is not
2. I'm	I am	you are
3. you'll	you will	I have
4. you're	you are	I am
5. isn't	is not	you will
6. wasn't	was not	were not
7. weren't	were not	he will
8. he'll	he will	who is
9. who's	who is	she will
10. she'll	she will	was not
11. we've	we have	will not
12. we'll	we will	they will
13. they'll	they will	we have
14. won't	will not	did not
15. didn't	did not	we will
16. I'd	I would	can not
17. they've	they have	let us
18. there's	there is	I would
19. let's	let us	they have
20. can't	can not	there is

© Mark Twain Media, Inc., Publisher 64

Phonics and Vocabulary Skills: Grade 4 — Identifying Contractions in Sentences

Name: Date:

Learning About Contractions: *Identifying Contractions in Sentences*

Read each of the following sentences. First, circle the contraction in each sentence. Then write the word pair the contraction stands for on the lines in (a). Next, find the words in the sentence indicated by the clues and write those words on the lines provided.

1. I'm not the one who broke the window.
   (a) contraction word pair: I am
   (b) word beginning with a blend, has a long "o" sound and silent "e": broke
2. She'll clean the room.
   (a) contraction word pair: She will, shall
   (b) word beginning with a blend, has a long "e" sound: clean
3. I'll bait the hook.
   (a) contraction word pair: I will, shall
   (b) word with a long "a" sound: bait
   (c) word that rhymes with book: hook
4. Isn't it time to eat the cheese?
   (a) contraction word pair: Is not
   (b) word with the long "i" sound and a silent "e": time
   (c) word with the long "e" sound and a silent "e": cheese
5. He'll boast that he won the game.
   (a) contraction word pair: He will, shall
   (b) word with the long "o" sound: boast
   (c) word with the long "a" sound and a silent "e": game
6. Who's the cool guy with the gray wool coat?
   (a) contraction word pair: Who is, was
   (b) word that rhymes with tool: cool
   (c) word with the same "oo" sound as took: wool
   (d) word with the long "a" sound: gray
   (e) word with the long "o" sound: coat
7. They'll need a pail, nail, spade, and rule.
   (a) contraction word pair: They will, shall
   (b) two rhyming words with the long "a" sound: pail nail
   (c) word with the long "a" sound and a silent "e": spade
   (d) word with the long "u" sound and a silent "e": rule

© Mark Twain Media, Inc., Publisher 66

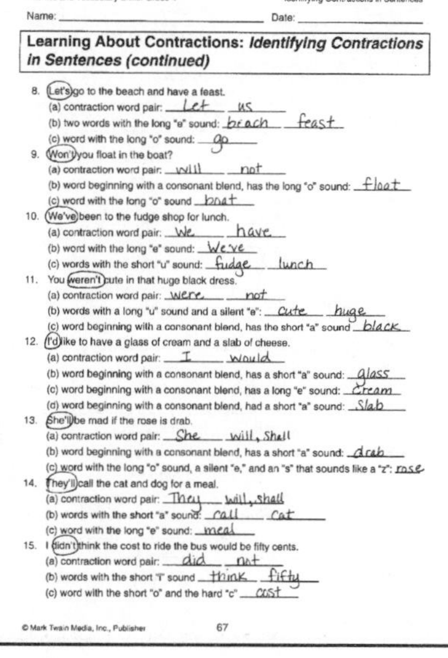
Phonics and Vocabulary Skills: Grade 4 — Identifying Contractions in Sentences

Name: Date:

Learning About Contractions: *Identifying Contractions in Sentences (continued)*

8. Let's go to the beach and have a feast.
   (a) contraction word pair: Let us
   (b) two words with the long "e" sound: beach feast
   (c) word with the long "o" sound: go
9. Won't you float in the boat?
   (a) contraction word pair: will not
   (b) word beginning with a consonant blend, has the long "o" sound: float
   (c) word with the long "o" sound: boat
10. We've been to the fudge shop for lunch.
   (a) contraction word pair: We have
   (b) word with the long "e" sound: We've
   (c) words with the short "u" sound: fudge lunch
11. You weren't cute in that huge black dress.
   (a) contraction word pair: were not
   (b) words with a long "u" sound and a silent "e": cute huge
   (c) word beginning with a consonant blend, has the short "a" sound: black
12. I'd like to have a glass of cream and a slab of cheese.
   (a) contraction word pair: I would
   (b) word beginning with a consonant blend, has a short "a" sound: glass
   (c) word beginning with a consonant blend, has a long "e" sound: cream
   (d) word beginning with a consonant blend, had a short "a" sound: slab
13. She'll be mad if the rose is drab.
   (a) contraction word pair: She will, shall
   (b) word beginning with a consonant blend, has a short "a" sound: drab
   (c) word with the long "o" sound, a silent "e," and an "s" that sounds like a "z": rose
14. They'll call the cat and dog for a meal.
   (a) contraction word pair: They will, shall
   (b) words with the short "a" sound: call cat
   (c) word with the long "e" sound: meal
15. I didn't think the cost to ride the bus would be fifty cents.
   (a) contraction word pair: did not
   (b) words with the short "i" sound: think fifty
   (c) word with the short "o" and the hard "c": cost

© Mark Twain Media, Inc., Publisher 67

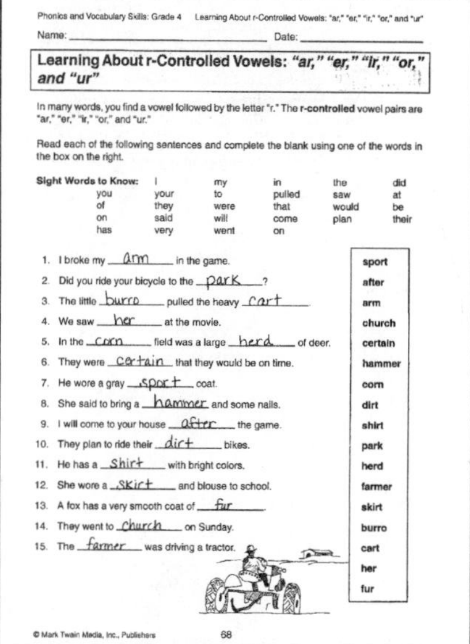
Phonics and Vocabulary Skills: Grade 4 — Learning About r-Controlled Vowels: "ar," "er," "ir," "or," and "ur"

Name: Date:

Learning About r-Controlled Vowels: "ar," "er," "ir," "or," and "ur"

In many words, you find a vowel followed by the letter "r." The **r-controlled** vowel pairs are "ar," "er," "ir," "or," and "ur."

Read each of the following sentences and complete the blank using one of the words in the box on the right.

Sight Words to Know: I, my, in, the, did, you, your, to, pulled, saw, at, of, they, were, that, would, be, on, said, will, come, plan, their, has, very, went, on

1. I broke my arm in the game.
2. Did you ride your bicycle to the park?
3. The little burro pulled the heavy cart.
4. We saw her at the movie.
5. In the corn field was a large herd of deer.
6. They were certain that they would be on time.
7. He wore a gray sport coat.
8. She said to bring a hammer and some nails.
9. I will come to your house after the game.
10. They plan to ride their dirt bikes.
11. He has a shirt with bright colors.
12. She wore a skirt and blouse to school.
13. A fox has a very smooth coat of fur.
14. They went to church on Sunday.
15. The farmer was driving a tractor.

sport, after, arm, church, certain, hammer, corn, dirt, shirt, park, herd, farmer, skirt, burro, cart, her, fur

© Mark Twain Media, Inc., Publishers 68

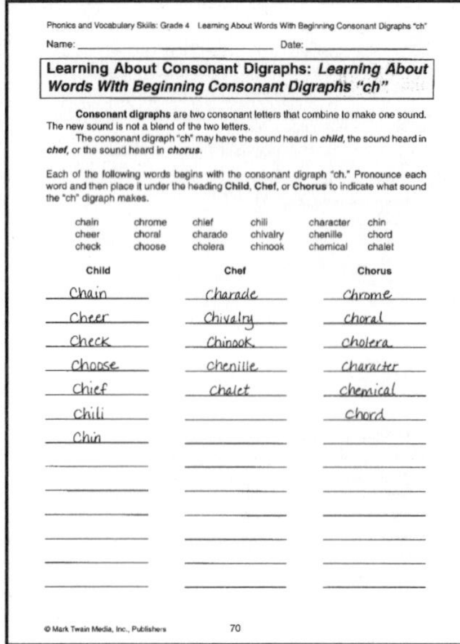

Phonics and Vocabulary Skills: Grade 4 Learning About Words With Beginning Consonant Digraphs "ch"

Name: ______ Date: ______

Learning About Consonant Digraphs: *Learning About Words With Beginning Consonant Digraphs "ch"*

Consonant digraphs are two consonant letters that combine to make one sound. The new sound is not a blend of the two letters.

The consonant digraph "ch" may have the sound heard in ***child***, the sound heard in ***chef***, or the sound heard in ***chorus***.

Each of the following words begins with the consonant digraph "ch." Pronounce each word and then place it under the heading **Child**, **Chef**, or **Chorus** to indicate what sound the "ch" digraph makes.

chain	chrome	chief	chili	character	chin
cheer	choral	charade	chivalry	chenille	chord
check	choose	cholera	chinook	chemical	chalet

Child	Chef	Chorus
Chain	Charade	Chrome
Cheer	Chivalry	Choral
Check	Chinook	Cholera
Choose	Chenille	Character
Chief	Chalet	Chemical
Chili		Chord
Chin		

© Mark Twain Media, Inc., Publishers 70

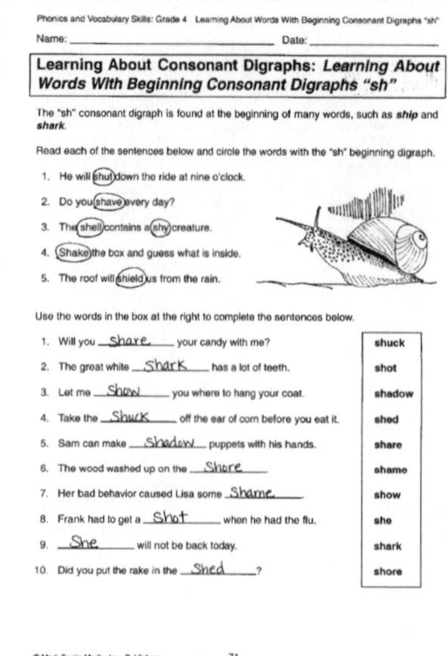

Phonics and Vocabulary Skills: Grade 4 Learning About Words With Beginning Consonant Digraphs "sh"

Name: ______ Date: ______

Learning About Consonant Digraphs: *Learning About Words With Beginning Consonant Digraphs "sh"*

The "sh" consonant digraph is found at the beginning of many words, such as ***ship*** and ***shark***.

Read each of the sentences below and circle the words with the "sh" beginning digraph.

1. He will (shut) down the ride at nine o'clock.
2. Do you (shave) every day?
3. The (shell) contains a (shy) creature.
4. (Shake) the box and guess what is inside.
5. The roof will (shield) us from the rain.

Use the words in the box at the right to complete the sentences below.

1. Will you share your candy with me?
2. The great white Shark has a lot of teeth.
3. Let me Show you where to hang your coat.
4. Take the Shuck off the ear of corn before you eat it.
5. Sam can make Shadow puppets with his hands.
6. The wood washed up on the Shore.
7. Her bad behavior caused Lisa some Shame.
8. Frank had to get a Shot when he had the flu.
9. She will not be back today.
10. Did you put the rake in the Shed?

shuck
shot
shadow
shed
share
shame
show
she
shark
shore

© Mark Twain Media, Inc., Publishers 71

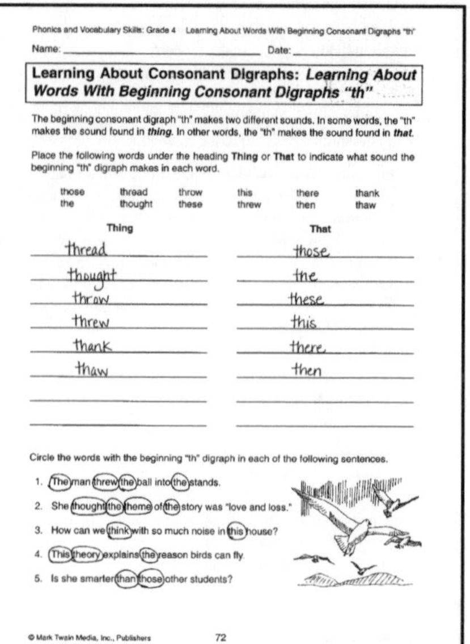

Phonics and Vocabulary Skills: Grade 4 Learning About Words With Beginning Consonant Digraphs "th"

Name: ______ Date: ______

Learning About Consonant Digraphs: *Learning About Words With Beginning Consonant Digraphs "th"*

The beginning consonant digraph "th" makes two different sounds. In some words, the "th" makes the sound found in ***thing***. In other words, the "th" makes the sound found in ***that***.

Place the following words under the heading **Thing** or **That** to indicate what sound the beginning "th" digraph makes in each word.

those	thread	throw	this	there	thank
the	thought	these	threw	then	thaw

Thing	That
thread	those
thought	the
throw	these
threw	this
thank	there
thaw	then

Circle the words with the beginning "th" digraph in each of the following sentences.

1. (The) man (threw) (the) ball into (the) stands.
2. She (thought) (the) (theme) of (the) story was "love and loss."
3. How can we (think) with so much noise in (this) house?
4. (This) (theory) (explains) (the) reason birds can fly.
5. Is she smarter (than) (those) other students?

© Mark Twain Media, Inc., Publishers 72

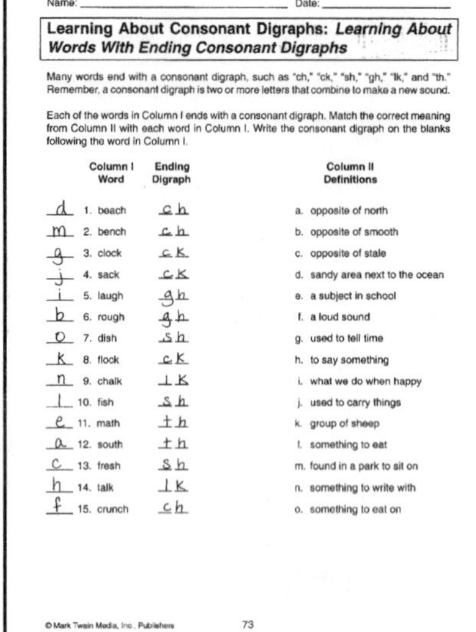

Phonics and Vocabulary Skills: Grade 4 Learning About Words With Ending Consonant Digraphs

Name: ______ Date: ______

Learning About Consonant Digraphs: *Learning About Words With Ending Consonant Digraphs*

Many words end with a consonant digraph, such as "ch," "ck," "sh," "gh," "lk," and "th." Remember, a consonant digraph is two or more letters that combine to make a new sound.

Each of the words in Column I ends with a consonant digraph. Match the correct meaning from Column II with each word in Column I. Write the consonant digraph on the blanks following the word in Column I.

	Column I Word	Ending Digraph	Column II Definitions
d	1. beach	ch	a. opposite of north
m	2. bench	ch	b. opposite of smooth
g	3. clock	ck	c. opposite of stale
j	4. sack	ck	d. sandy area next to the ocean
i	5. laugh	gh	e. a subject in school
b	6. rough	gh	f. a loud sound
o	7. dish	sh	g. used to tell time
k	8. flock	ck	h. to say something
n	9. chalk	lk	i. what we do when happy
l	10. fish	sh	j. used to carry things
e	11. math	th	k. group of sheep
a	12. south	th	l. something to eat
c	13. fresh	sh	m. found in a park to sit on
h	14. talk	lk	n. something to write with
f	15. crunch	ch	o. something to eat on

© Mark Twain Media, Inc., Publishers 73

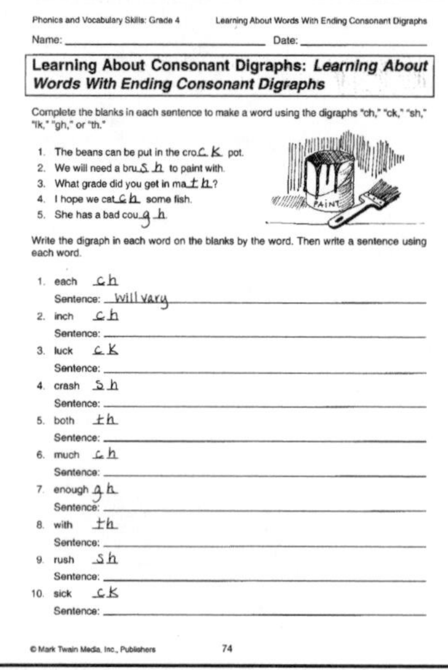

Phonics and Vocabulary Skills: Grade 4 Learning About Words With Ending Consonant Digraphs

Name: ______ Date: ______

Learning About Consonant Digraphs: *Learning About Words With Ending Consonant Digraphs*

Complete the blanks in each sentence to make a word using the digraphs "ch," "ck," "sh," "lk," "gh," or "th."

1. The beans can be put in the croCK pot.
2. We will need a bruSh to paint with.
3. What grade did you get in mat h?
4. I hope we catch some fish.
5. She has a bad cough.

Write the digraph in each word on the blanks by the word. Then write a sentence using each word.

1. each ch
   Sentence: will vary
2. inch ch
   Sentence:
3. luck ck
   Sentence:
4. crash sh
   Sentence:
5. both th
   Sentence:
6. much ch
   Sentence:
7. enough gh
   Sentence:
8. with th
   Sentence:
9. rush sh
   Sentence:
10. sick ck
    Sentence:

© Mark Twain Media, Inc., Publishers 74

Phonics and Vocabulary Skills: Grade 4 Learning About The Digraph "ph"

Name: ______ Date: ______

Learning About Consonant Digraphs: *Learning About the Digraph "ph"*

When the consonant digraph **"ph"** is found in a word, it is pronounced as **/f/**. In the word ***phone***, the letters "ph" are pronounced as **/f/**. **Phone** is pronounced as **fone** with a long "o" and a silent "e."

Read each of the following sentences. Find the words with the digraph "ph." Draw a slash through the "ph" and write the word on the blank with the letter "f" replacing the "ph."

Sight Words to Know:	the	is	there	on	table
	of	my	if	we	are	going
	to	take	second	so	am	his

1. The phone is ringing. fone
2. There on the table is a photo of my sister. foto
3. If we are going to play football, we must take a physical. fysical
4. The moon is in the second phase. fase
5. He is my uncle, so I am his nephew. nefew

In each of the following words, the letters "ph" are pronounced with the sound of "f." Write each word in the **"ph" Deleted** column and place a slash through the "ph." Then write the pronunciation of the word in the **Pronunciation** column. Finally, write a sentence using each "ph" word.

Word	"ph" Deleted	Pronunciation
1. phone	phone	fone
Sentence: will vary		
2. phrase	phrase	frase
Sentence:		
3. nephew	nephew	nefew
Sentence:		
4. graph	graph	graf
Sentence:		
5. phonics	phonics	fonics
Sentence:		

© Mark Twain Media, Inc., Publishers 75

Phonics and Vocabulary Skills: Grade 4 Learning About The Digraph "gh"

Name: ______ Date: ______

Learning About Consonant Digraphs: *Learning About the Digraph "gh"*

When the letters **"gh"** come at the end of a word, the "gh" is pronounced as **/f/**. In the word ***laugh***, the letters "gh" are pronounced as an **/f/** sound. **Laugh** is pronounced as **laf** with the short sound of "a."

Read each of the following sentences. Find the words with the digraph "gh" and draw a line through the "gh." Then write the word on the blank with the letter "f" replacing the "gh."

Sight Words to Know:	he	is	will	very	there
	guy	cake	from	was	loud	been
	sick	on	that	car	road	

1. He is a very tough guy. tuf
2. Will there be enough cake for all of us? enouf
3. The laughter from the next room was very loud. laufter
4. He has been sick and has a bad cough. couf
5. We drove the car on a road that was quite rough. rouf

In each of the following words, the digraph "gh" is pronounced with the sound of "f." Write each word in the **"gh" Deleted** column and draw a slash through the "gh." Then write the pronunciation of the word in the **Pronunciation** column. Finally, write a sentence using each "gh" word.

Word	"gh" Deleted	Pronunciation
1. laugh	laugh	laf
Sentence: will vary		
2. rough	rough	ruf
Sentence:		
3. tough	tough	tuf
Sentence:		
4. laughter	laughter	lafter
Sentence:		
5. enough	enough	enuf
Sentence:		

© Mark Twain Media, Inc., Publishers 76

Phonics and Vocabulary Skills: Grade 4 Silent "k"

Name: ______ Date: ______

Learning About Words With Silent Letters: *Silent "k"*

Many words have letters that are silent. In words that begin with the letters **"kn,"** the **"k"** is silent. For example, ***knew*** is pronounced ***new***. The "k" is silent.

In each of the following words, the "k" is silent. Write the word in the **Silent "k"** column and draw a slash through the "k" to show that it is silent. Then write the pronunciation of the word in the **Pronunciation** column. Finally, write a sentence using the word.

Word	Silent "k"	Pronunciation
1. knew	knew	new
Sentence: will vary		
2. knife	knife	nife
Sentence:		
3. knit	Knit	nit
Sentence:		
4. knob	Knob	nob
Sentence:		
5. knee	Knee	nee
Sentence:		
6. knot	Knot	not
Sentence:		
7. knock	Knock	nock
Sentence:		
8. kneel	Kneel	neel
Sentence:		
9. knack	Knack	nack
Sentence:		
10. knead	Knead	nead
Sentence:		

© Mark Twain Media, Inc., Publishers 77

Phonics and Vocabulary Skills: Grade 4 Silent "gh"

Name: ______ Date: ______

Learning About Words With Silent Letters: *Silent "gh"*

In some words, the letters **"gh"** are silent. For example, ***night*** is pronounced ***nit*** with a long "i" sound. The "gh" is silent.

In each of the following words, the "gh" is silent. Write the word in the **Silent "gh"** column and draw a slash through the "gh" to show that it is silent. Then write the pronunciation of the word in the **Pronunciation** column, using the macron symbol (¯) for long vowels where appropriate. Finally, write a sentence using the word.

Word	Silent "gh"	Pronunciation
1. night	night	nīt
Sentence: will vary		
2. light	light	līt
Sentence:		
3. fight	fight	fīt
Sentence:		
4. might	might	mīt
Sentence:		
5. sight	sight	sīt
Sentence:		
6. bright	bright	brīt
Sentence:		
7. thought	thought	thot
Sentence:		
8. through	through	thrū
Sentence:		
9. brought	brought	brot
Sentence:		
10. caught	caught	cot
Sentence:		

© Mark Twain Media, Inc., Publishers 78

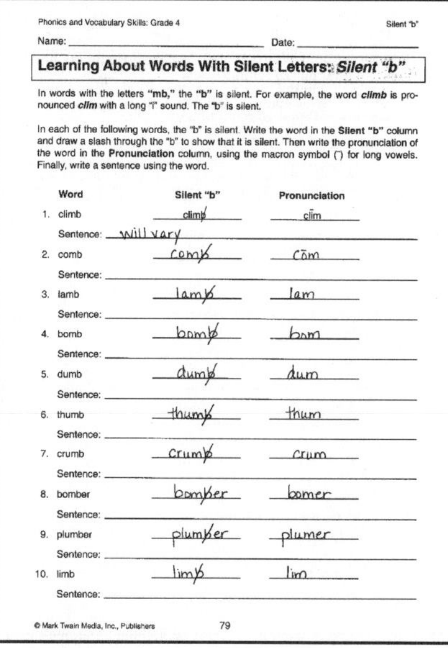

Phonics and Vocabulary Skills: Grade 4 — Silent "b"

Name: ______ Date: ______

Learning About Words With Silent Letters: *Silent "b"*

In words with the letters **"mb,"** the **"b"** is silent. For example, the word ***climb*** is pronounced ***clim*** with a long "i" sound. The "b" is silent.

In each of the following words, the "b" is silent. Write the word in the **Silent "b"** column and draw a slash through the "b" to show that it is silent. Then write the pronunciation of the word in the **Pronunciation** column, using the macron symbol (¯) for long vowels. Finally, write a sentence using the word.

	Word	Silent "b"	Pronunciation
1.	climb	climb̸	clīm
	Sentence: will vary		
2.	comb	comb̸	cōm
3.	lamb	lamb̸	lam
4.	bomb	bomb̸	bom
5.	dumb	dumb̸	dum
6.	thumb	thumb̸	thum
7.	crumb	crumb̸	crum
8.	bomber	bomb̸er	bomer
9.	plumber	plumb̸er	plumer
10.	limb	limb̸	lim

© Mark Twain Media, Inc., Publishers 79

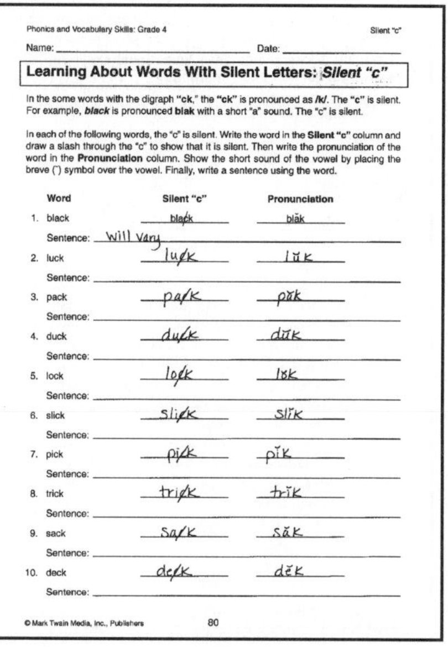

Phonics and Vocabulary Skills: Grade 4 — Silent "c"

Name: ______ Date: ______

Learning About Words With Silent Letters: *Silent "c"*

In the some words with the digraph **"ck,"** the **"ck"** is pronounced as **/k/**. The **"c"** is silent. For example, ***black*** is pronounced **blak** with a short "a" sound. The "c" is silent.

In each of the following words, the "c" is silent. Write the word in the **Silent "c"** column and draw a slash through the "c" to show that it is silent. Then write the pronunciation of the word in the **Pronunciation** column. Show the short sound of the vowel by placing the breve (˘) symbol over the vowel. Finally, write a sentence using the word.

	Word	Silent "c"	Pronunciation
1.	black	blac̸k	blăk
	Sentence: will vary		
2.	luck	luc̸k	lŭk
3.	pack	pac̸k	păk
4.	duck	duc̸k	dŭk
5.	lock	loc̸k	lŏk
6.	slick	slic̸k	slĭk
7.	pick	pic̸k	pĭk
8.	trick	tric̸k	trĭk
9.	sack	sac̸k	săk
10.	deck	dec̸k	dĕk

© Mark Twain Media, Inc., Publishers 80

Phonics and Vocabulary Skills: Grade 4 — Silent "w"

Name: ______ Date: ______

Learning About Words With Silent Letters: *Silent "w"*

In words with the **"wr"** letter combination, the **"w"** is silent. For example, ***write*** is pronounced as ***rite*** with a long "i" sound. The "w" is silent.

In each of the following words, the "w" is silent. Write the word in the **Silent "w"** column and draw a slash through the "w" to show that it is silent. Then write the pronunciation of the word in the **Pronunciation** column. Use the macron (¯) symbol to indicate a long vowel sound and a breve (˘) symbol to indicate a short vowel sound. If there is a silent "e," draw a slash mark through it. Finally, write a sentence using the word.

	Word	Silent "w"	Pronunciation
1.	write	w̸rite	rīte̸
	Sentence: will vary		
2.	wrote	w̸rote	rōte̸
3.	wrong	w̸rong	rŏng
4.	wreck	w̸reck	rĕk
5.	wrap	w̸rap	răp
6.	wrist	w̸rist	rĭst
7.	wring	w̸ring	rĭng
8.	wrench	w̸rench	rĕnch
9.	wreath	w̸reath	rēth
10.	wren	w̸ren	rĕn

© Mark Twain Media, Inc., Publishers 81

Phonics and Vocabulary Skills: Grade 4 — Reviewing What Has Been Learned

Name: ______ Date: ______

Learning About Words With Silent Letters: Reviewing What Has Been Learned

Circle all of the words with silent consonant letters. Then write the words below in the **Words With Silent Letters** column. Finally, write the pronunciation of the words in the **Pronunciation of Words** column.

Sam heard the (knock) at the door. He looked at the (clock) and (knew) it was time to leave for the game. He turned the (knob) on the door and there stood his friend John with a (wrap) around his (right) (wrist). In his left hand, John had a (sack) with a (light) coat.

"Time to leave for the game," said John.

Sam gave him a (knowing) smile. "I need to (write) a note to mother," said Sam.

Sam opened the door again and remembered that there (might) be a photo after the game, so he would need a (comb). He placed the (black) (comb) in the pocket of his raincoat.

A (light) rain began to fall as the game began. It was a (tough) game with (rough) play. It took a (trick) play and a pass that John (caught) to win the game. Even (though) he had a (cough) and a sore (thumb), John was able to smile for the photograph.

Words With Silent Letters	Pronunciation of Words	Words With Silent Letters	Pronunciation of Words
knock	nŏk	black	blăk
clock	clŏk	com	cōm
knew	new	light	līt
knob	nŏb	tough	tŭf
wrap	răp	rough	rŭf
right	rīt	trick	trĭk
wrist	rĭst	caught	cŏt
sack	săk	though	thō
light	līt	cough	cŏf
knowing	nōwing	thumb	thŭm
write	rīt		
might	mīt		
comb	cōm		

© Mark Twain Media, Inc., Publishers 82

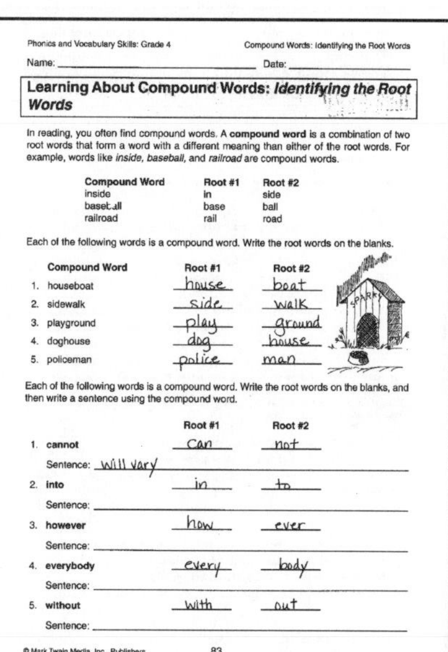

Phonics and Vocabulary Skills: Grade 4 — Compound Words: Identifying the Root Words

Name: ______ Date: ______

Learning About Compound Words: *Identifying the Root Words*

In reading, you often find compound words. A **compound word** is a combination of two root words that form a word with a different meaning than either of the root words. For example, words like *inside, baseball,* and *railroad* are compound words.

Compound Word	Root #1	Root #2
inside	in	side
baseball	base	ball
railroad	rail	road

Each of the following words is a compound word. Write the root words on the blanks.

	Compound Word	Root #1	Root #2
1.	houseboat	house	boat
2.	sidewalk	side	walk
3.	playground	play	ground
4.	doghouse	dog	house
5.	policeman	police	man

Each of the following words is a compound word. Write the root words on the blanks, and then write a sentence using the compound word.

		Root #1	Root #2
1.	**cannot**	can	not
	Sentence: will vary		
2.	**into**	in	to
3.	**however**	how	ever
4.	**everybody**	every	body
5.	**without**	with	out

© Mark Twain Media, Inc., Publishers 83

Phonics and Vocabulary Skills: Grade 4 — Using Compound Words in Sentences

Name: ______ Date: ______

Learning About Compound Words: *Using Compound Words in Sentences*

Complete the blanks in the following sentences by using the compound words from the box below. Write the correct word on the blank.

Sight Words to Know: he, put, the, in, on, each, of, us, must, take, will, get, can, and, you, some, plan, to, were, by, it, so

earthquake	**paintbrush**	**suitcase**	**sunset**	**snowman**
fireplace	**campfire**	**afternoon**	**mailbox**	**raincoat**

1. He put the letters in the mailbox.
2. Each of us must take a suitcase on the trip.
3. We will get the can of paint, and you can get the paintbrush.
4. I will get some wood to start a fire in the fireplace.
5. We do not plan to leave until late afternoon.
6. After the meal, we sat around the campfire and sang songs.
7. Many buildings were destroyed by the earthquake.
8. It looks like rain, so you'd better take your raincoat.
9. After the snow stopped, we went out and built a snowman.
10. We sat on the beach and watched the beautiful sunset.

Use each of the following compound words in a sentence.

1. pancake: sentences will vary
2. sailboat:
3. railroad:
4. grandfather:
5. moonlight:

© Mark Twain Media, Inc., Publishers 84

Phonics and Vocabulary Skills: Grade 4 — Adding "ing" to Words That End in a Consonant

Name: ______ Date: ______

Learning About Words With Inflectional Endings: *Adding "ing" to Words That End in a Consonant*

An **inflection** is a letter or letters added at the end of a root word that changes the grammatical function of the word. Examples of inflections are "ing," "'s," "es," "s," "ed," "er," and "est."

Many words end with "ing." To add "ing" to words ending with a single consonant, you usually double the last consonant and then add "ing."

Examples: beg = begging pat = patting

Complete each of the following blanks and make a new word by adding "ing." Write a sentence using the new "ing" word.

	Base Word	Double the Final Consonant	Add "ing" to Make a New Word
1.	run	runn	running
	Sentence: will vary		
2.	fan	fann	fanning
3.	hit	hitt	hitting
4.	hop	hopp	hopping
5.	hug	hugg	hugging
6.	nag	nagg	nagging
7.	plan	plann	planning
8.	jog	jogg	jogging
9.	pet	pett	petting
10.	shop	shopp	shopping

© Mark Twain Media, Inc., Publishers 85

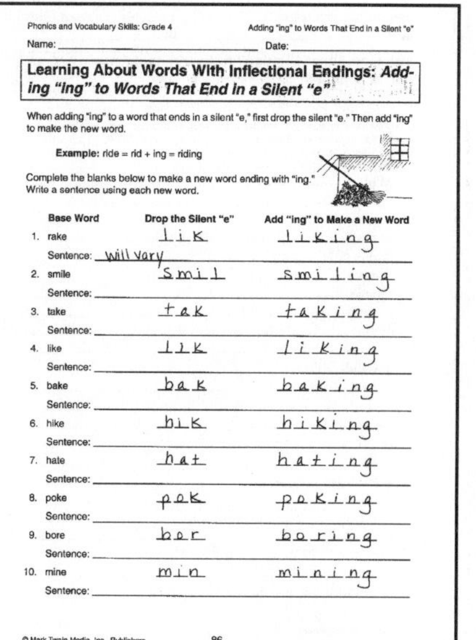

Phonics and Vocabulary Skills: Grade 4 — Adding "ing" to Words That End in a Silent "e"

Name: ______ Date: ______

Learning About Words With Inflectional Endings: *Adding "ing" to Words That End in a Silent "e"*

When adding "ing" to a word that ends in a silent "e," first drop the silent "e." Then add "ing" to make the new word.

Example: ride = rid + ing = riding

Complete the blanks below to make a new word ending with "ing." Write a sentence using each new word.

	Base Word	Drop the Silent "e"	Add "ing" to Make a New Word
1.	rake	lik	liking
	Sentence: will vary		
2.	smile	smil	smiling
3.	take	tak	taking
4.	like	lik	liking
5.	bake	bak	baking
6.	hike	hik	hiking
7.	hate	hat	hating
8.	poke	pok	poking
9.	bore	bor	boring
10.	mine	min	mining

© Mark Twain Media, Inc., Publishers 86

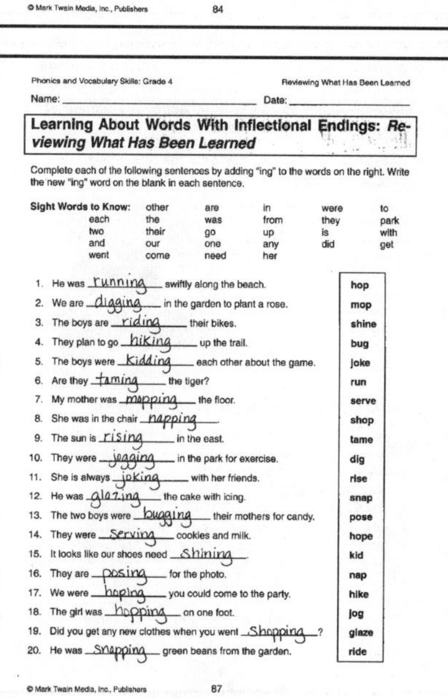

Phonics and Vocabulary Skills: Grade 4 — Reviewing What Has Been Learned

Name: ______ Date: ______

Learning About Words With Inflectional Endings: *Reviewing What Has Been Learned*

Complete each of the following sentences by adding "ing" to the words on the right. Write the new "ing" word on the blank in each sentence.

Sight Words to Know: other, are, in, were, to, each, the, was, from, they, park, two, their, go, up, is, with, and, our, one, any, did, get, went, come, need, her

1. He was running swiftly along the beach. — **hop**
2. We are digging in the garden to plant a rose. — **mop**
3. The boys are riding their bikes. — **shine**
4. They plan to go hiking up the trail. — **bug**
5. The boys were kidding each other about the game. — **joke**
6. Are they taming the tiger? — **run**
7. My mother was mopping the floor. — **serve**
8. She was in the chair napping. — **shop**
9. The sun is rising in the east. — **tame**
10. They were jogging in the park for exercise. — **dig**
11. She is always joking with her friends. — **rise**
12. He was glazing the cake with icing. — **snap**
13. The two boys were bugging their mothers for candy. — **pose**
14. They were serving cookies and milk. — **hope**
15. It looks like our shoes need shining. — **kid**
16. They are posing for the photo. — **nap**
17. We were hoping you could come to the party. — **hike**
18. The girl was hopping on one foot. — **jog**
19. Did you get any new clothes when you went shopping? — **glaze**
20. He was snapping green beans from the garden. — **ride**

© Mark Twain Media, Inc., Publishers 87

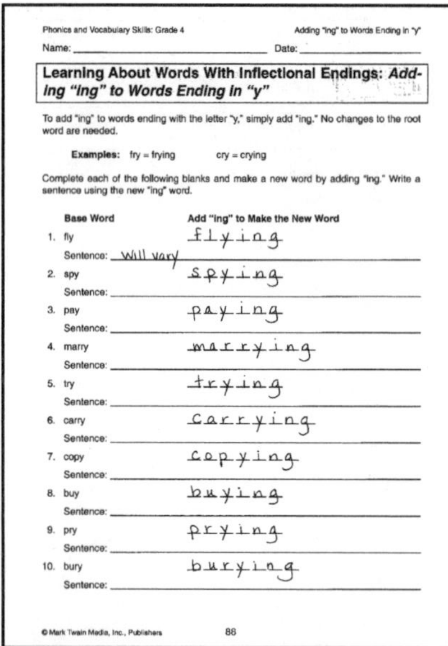
Phonics and Vocabulary Skills: Grade 4 Adding "ing" to Words Ending in "y"

Name: Date:

Learning About Words With Inflectional Endings: *Adding "ing" to Words Ending in "y"*

To add "ing" to words ending with the letter "y," simply add "ing." No changes to the root word are needed.

Examples: fry = frying cry = crying

Complete each of the following blanks and make a new word by adding "ing." Write a sentence using the new "ing" word.

	Base Word	Add "ing" to Make the New Word
1.	fly	flying
	Sentence: will vary	
2.	spy	spying
3.	pay	paying
4.	marry	marrying
5.	try	trying
6.	carry	carrying
7.	copy	copying
8.	buy	buying
9.	pry	prying
10.	bury	burying

© Mark Twain Media, Inc., Publishers 88

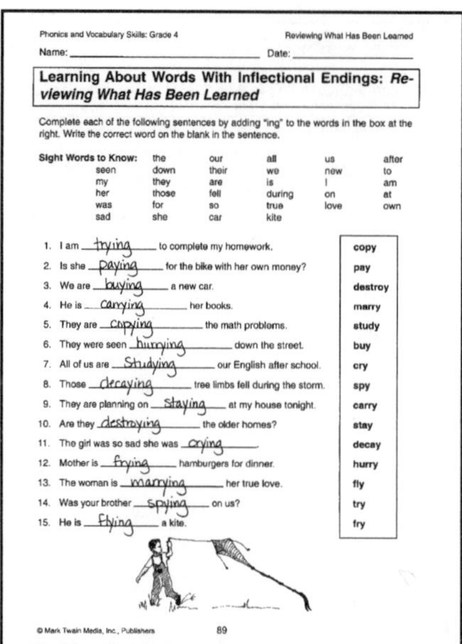
Phonics and Vocabulary Skills: Grade 4 Reviewing What Has Been Learned

Name: Date:

Learning About Words With Inflectional Endings: *Reviewing What Has Been Learned*

Complete each of the following sentences by adding "ing" to the words in the box at the right. Write the correct word on the blank in the sentence.

Sight Words to Know: the, seen, my, her, was, sad, our, down, they, those, for, she, all, their, are, fell, so, car, us, we, is, during, true, kite, after, new, I, on, love, to, am, at, own

1. I am trying to complete my homework.
2. Is she paying for the bike with her own money?
3. We are buying a new car.
4. He is carrying her books.
5. They are copying the math problems.
6. They were seen hurrying down the street.
7. All of us are studying our English after school.
8. Those decaying tree limbs fell during the storm.
9. They are planning on staying at my house tonight.
10. Are they destroying the older homes?
11. The girl was so sad she was crying.
12. Mother is frying hamburgers for dinner.
13. The woman is marrying her true love.
14. Was your brother spying on us?
15. He is flying a kite.

Box: copy, pay, destroy, marry, study, buy, cry, spy, carry, stay, decay, hurry, fly, try, fry

© Mark Twain Media, Inc., Publishers 89

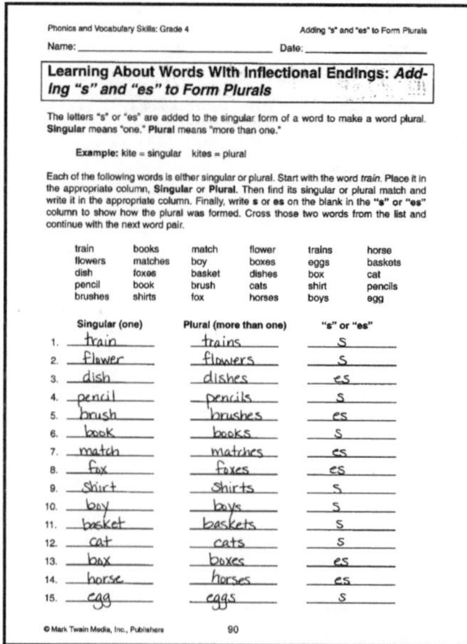
Phonics and Vocabulary Skills: Grade 4 Adding "s" and "es" to Form Plurals

Name: Date:

Learning About Words With Inflectional Endings: *Adding "s" and "es" to Form Plurals*

The letters "s" or "es" are added to the singular form of a word to make a word plural. **Singular** means "one." **Plural** means "more than one."

Example: kite = singular kites = plural

Each of the following words is either singular or plural. Start with the word *train*. Place it in the appropriate column, **Singular** or **Plural**. Then find its singular or plural match and write it in the appropriate column. Finally, write **s** or **es** on the blank in the **"s" or "es"** column to show how the plural was formed. Cross those two words from the list and continue with the next word pair.

train, flowers, dish, pencil, brushes, books, matches, foxes, book, shirts, match, boy, basket, brush, fox, flower, boxes, dishes, cats, horses, trains, eggs, box, shirt, boys, horse, baskets, cat, pencils, egg

	Singular (one)	Plural (more than one)	"s" or "es"
1.	train	trains	s
2.	flower	flowers	s
3.	dish	dishes	es
4.	pencil	pencils	s
5.	brush	brushes	es
6.	book	books	s
7.	match	matches	es
8.	fox	foxes	es
9.	shirt	shirts	s
10.	boy	boys	s
11.	basket	baskets	s
12.	cat	cats	s
13.	box	boxes	es
14.	horse	horses	es
15.	egg	eggs	s

© Mark Twain Media, Inc., Publishers 90

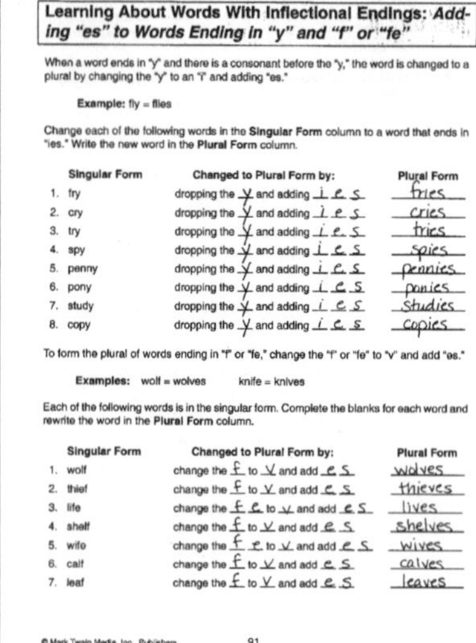
Phonics and Vocabulary Skills: Grade 4 Adding "es" to Words Ending in "y" and "f" or "fe"

Name: Date:

Learning About Words With Inflectional Endings: *Adding "es" to Words Ending in "y" and "f" or "fe"*

When a word ends in "y" and there is a consonant before the "y," the word is changed to a plural by changing the "y" to an "i" and adding "es."

Example: fly = flies

Change each of the following words in the **Singular Form** column to a word that ends in "ies." Write the new word in the **Plural Form** column.

	Singular Form	Changed to Plural Form by:	Plural Form
1.	fry	dropping the y and adding ies	fries
2.	cry	dropping the y and adding ies	cries
3.	try	dropping the y and adding ies	tries
4.	spy	dropping the y and adding ies	spies
5.	penny	dropping the y and adding ies	pennies
6.	pony	dropping the y and adding ies	ponies
7.	study	dropping the y and adding ies	studies
8.	copy	dropping the y and adding ies	copies

To form the plural of words ending in "f" or "fe," change the "f" or "fe" to "v" and add "es."

Examples: wolf = wolves knife = knives

Each of the following words is in the singular form. Complete the blanks for each word and rewrite the word in the **Plural Form** column.

	Singular Form	Changed to Plural Form by:	Plural Form
1.	wolf	change the f to v and add es	wolves
2.	thief	change the f to v and add es	thieves
3.	life	change the fe to v and add es	lives
4.	shelf	change the f to v and add es	shelves
5.	wife	change the fe to v and add es	wives
6.	calf	change the f to v and add es	calves
7.	leaf	change the f to v and add es	leaves

© Mark Twain Media, Inc., Publishers 91

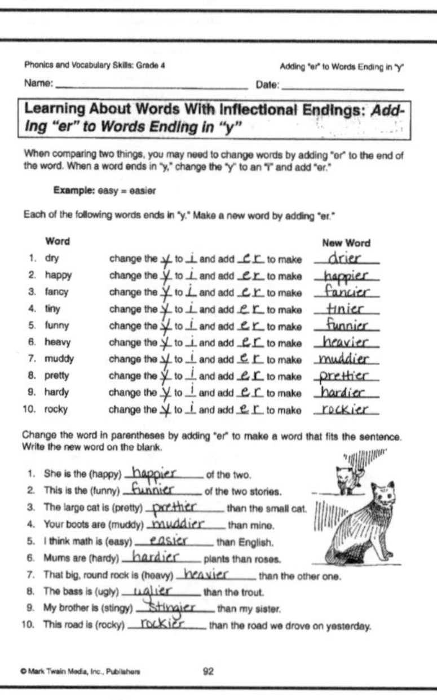
Phonics and Vocabulary Skills: Grade 4 Adding "er" to Words Ending in "y"

Name: Date:

Learning About Words With Inflectional Endings: *Adding "er" to Words Ending in "y"*

When comparing two things, you may need to change words by adding "er" to the end of the word. When a word ends in "y," change the "y" to an "i" and add "er."

Example: easy = easier

Each of the following words ends in "y." Make a new word by adding "er."

	Word		New Word
1.	dry	change the y to i and add er to make	drier
2.	happy	change the y to i and add er to make	happier
3.	fancy	change the y to i and add er to make	fancier
4.	tiny	change the y to i and add er to make	tinier
5.	funny	change the y to i and add er to make	funnier
6.	heavy	change the y to i and add er to make	heavier
7.	muddy	change the y to i and add er to make	muddier
8.	pretty	change the y to i and add er to make	prettier
9.	hardy	change the y to i and add er to make	hardier
10.	rocky	change the y to i and add er to make	rockier

Change the word in parentheses by adding "er" to make a word that fits the sentence. Write the new word on the blank.

1. She is the (happy) happier of the two.
2. This is the (funny) funnier of the two stories.
3. The large cat is (pretty) prettier than the small cat.
4. Your boots are (muddy) muddier than mine.
5. I think math is (easy) easier than English.
6. Mums are (hardy) hardier plants than roses.
7. That big, round rock is (heavy) heavier than the other one.
8. The bass is (ugly) uglier than the trout.
9. My brother is (stingy) stingier than my sister.
10. This road is (rocky) rockier than the road we drove on yesterday.

© Mark Twain Media, Inc., Publishers 92

Phonics and Vocabulary Skills: Grade 4 Adding "est" to Words Ending in "y"

Name: Date:

Learning About Words With Inflectional Endings: *Adding "est" to Words Ending in "y"*

When comparing three or more things, you may need to add "est" to a word. When a word ends in "y," change the "y" to an "i" and add "est."

Example: dry = driest

Each of the following words ends in "y." Make a new word by adding "est." Write a sentence using the new word you have made.

	Word		New Word
1.	dry	change the y to i and add est to make	driest
	Sentence: will vary		
2.	happy	change the y to i and add est to make	happiest
3.	fancy	change the y to i and add est to make	fanciest
4.	tiny	change the y to i and add est to make	tiniest
5.	funny	change the y to i and add est to make	funniest
6.	heavy	change the y to i and add est to make	heaviest
7.	muddy	change the y to i and add est to make	muddiest
8.	pretty	change the y to i and add est to make	prettiest
9.	hardy	change the y to i and add est to make	hardiest
10.	rocky	change the y to i and add est to make	rockiest

© Mark Twain Media, Inc., Publishers 93

Phonics and Vocabulary Skills: Grade 4 Reviewing What Has Been Learned

Name: Date:

Learning About Words With Inflectional Endings: *Reviewing What Has Been Learned*

Change each of the following words to a new word ending in "es."

	Word	New Word With "es" Ending
1.	party	parties
2.	quarry	quarries
3.	ferry	ferries
4.	query	queries
5.	candy	candies
6.	dwarf	dwarves
7.	sheaf	sheaves
8.	wharf	wharves
9.	hoof	hoofs or hooves
10.	loaf	loaves

Change each of the following words to a new word ending in "er" and "est."

	Word	New Word With "er" Ending	New Word With "est" Ending
1.	messy	messier	messiest
2.	fussy	fussier	fussiest
3.	crazy	crazier	craziest
4.	flimsy	flimsier	flimsiest
5.	mighty	mightier	mightiest
6.	squishy	squishier	squishiest
7.	friendly	friendlier	friendliest
8.	zany	zanier	zaniest
9.	lazy	lazier	laziest
10.	stringy	stringier	stringiest

© Mark Twain Media, Inc., Publishers 94

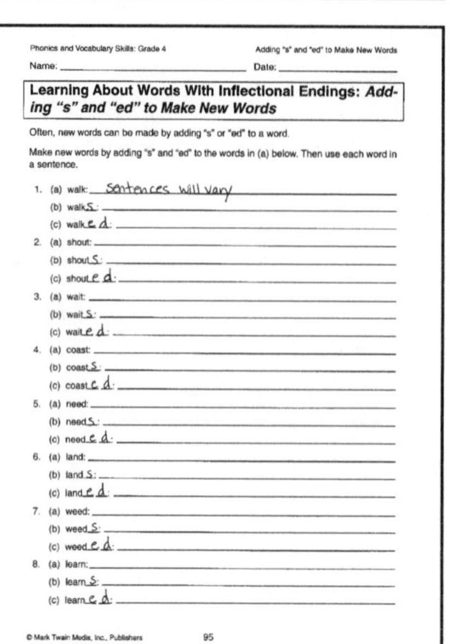
Phonics and Vocabulary Skills: Grade 4 Adding "s" and "ed" to Make New Words

Name: Date:

Learning About Words With Inflectional Endings: *Adding "s" and "ed" to Make New Words*

Often, new words can be made by adding "s" or "ed" to a word.

Make new words by adding "s" and "ed" to the words in (a) below. Then use each word in a sentence.

1. (a) walk: Sentences will vary
   (b) walks:
   (c) walked:
2. (a) shout: (b) shouts: (c) shouted:
3. (a) wait: (b) waits: (c) waited:
4. (a) coast: (b) coasts: (c) coasted:
5. (a) need: (b) needs: (c) needed:
6. (a) land: (b) lands: (c) landed:
7. (a) weed: (b) weeds: (c) weeded:
8. (a) learn: (b) learns: (c) learned:

© Mark Twain Media, Inc., Publishers 95

Phonics and Vocabulary Skills: Grade 4 Adding "s" and "ed" to Make New Words

Name: Date:

Learning About Words With Inflectional Endings: *Adding "s" and "ed" to Make New Words*

Complete each of the following sentences by using one of the three words following each sentence. Choose the word that makes sense in each sentence and write it on the blank.

1. Yesterday he planted the rose in the pot. plant plants planted
2. He will plant roses for his mother. plant plants planted
3. She plants roses each summer. plant plants planted
4. I waited all day for you to call. wait waits waited
5. He waits for her each day. wait waits waited
6. If I am late, don't wait for me. wait waits waited
7. We had a feast at the park. feast feasts feasted
8. Some people have many feasts each year. feast feasts feasted
9. She said that they feasted on turkey. feast feasts feasted
10. We pounded nails all day. pound pounds pounded
11. How many pounds are in the bag? pound pounds pounded
12. He ate a pound of grapes. pound pounds pounded
13. They use wood to heat the room. heat heats heated
14. It heats up each summer. heat heats heated
15. We had a heated talk about the game. heat heats heated
16. Sam combed his hair this morning. comb combs combed
17. Her comb is pink and blue. comb combs combed
18. He combs the lawn for weeds every week. comb combs combed
19. We were seated in the back of the car. seat seats seated
20. This bus seats 48 people. seat seats seated
21. Is this seat taken? seat seats seated

© Mark Twain Media, Inc., Publishers 96

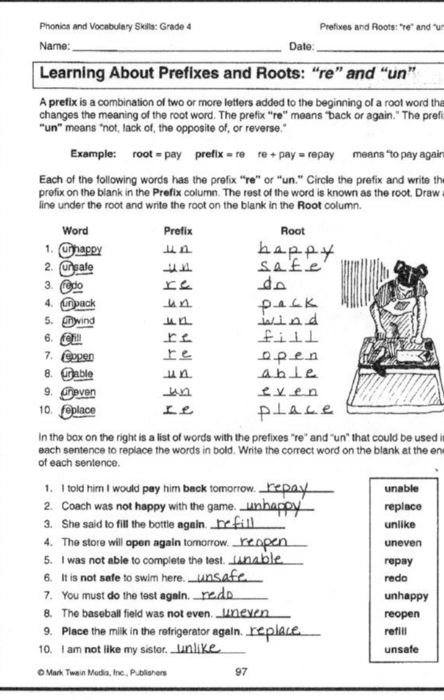
Phonics and Vocabulary Skills: Grade 4 Prefixes and Roots: "re" and "un"

Name: Date:

Learning About Prefixes and Roots: "re" and "un"

A **prefix** is a combination of two or more letters added to the beginning of a root word that changes the meaning of the root word. The prefix **"re"** means "back or again." The prefix **"un"** means "not, lack of, the opposite of, or reverse."

Example: root = pay prefix = re re + pay = repay means "to pay again"

Each of the following words has the prefix **"re"** or **"un."** Circle the prefix and write the prefix on the blank in the **Prefix** column. The rest of the word is known as the root. Draw a line under the root and write the root on the blank in the **Root** column.

Word	Prefix	Root
1. unhappy	un	happy
2. unsafe	un	safe
3. redo	re	do
4. unpack	un	pack
5. unwind	un	wind
6. refill	re	fill
7. reopen	re	open
8. unable	un	able
9. uneven	un	even
10. replace	re	place

In the box on the right is a list of words with the prefixes "re" and "un" that could be used in each sentence to replace the words in bold. Write the correct word on the blank at the end of each sentence.

1. I told him I would **pay** him **back** tomorrow. repay
2. Coach was **not happy** with the game. unhappy
3. She said to **fill** the bottle **again**. refill
4. The store will **open again** tomorrow. reopen
5. I was **not able** to complete the test. unable
6. It is **not safe** to swim here. unsafe
7. You must **do** the test **again**. redo
8. The baseball field was **not even**. uneven
9. **Place** the milk in the refrigerator **again**. replace
10. I am **not like** my sister. unlike

unable, replace, unlike, uneven, repay, redo, unhappy, reopen, refill, unsafe

© Mark Twain Media, Inc., Publishers 97

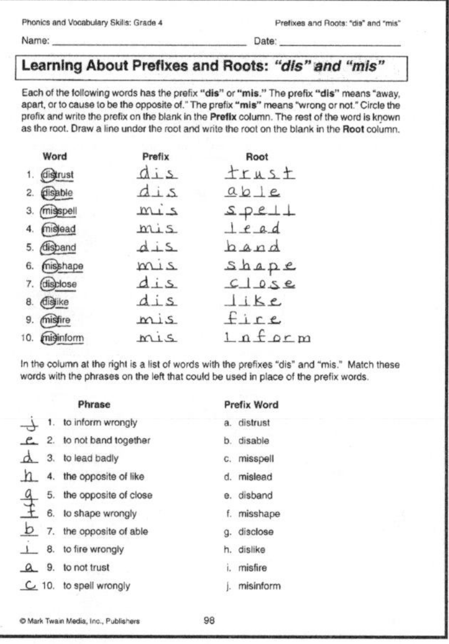
Phonics and Vocabulary Skills: Grade 4 Prefixes and Roots: "dis" and "mis"

Name: Date:

Learning About Prefixes and Roots: "dis" and "mis"

Each of the following words has the prefix **"dis"** or **"mis."** The prefix **"dis"** means "away, apart, or to cause to be the opposite of." The prefix **"mis"** means "wrong or not." Circle the prefix and write the prefix on the blank in the **Prefix** column. The rest of the word is known as the root. Draw a line under the root and write the root on the blank in the **Root** column.

Word	Prefix	Root
1. distrust	dis	trust
2. disable	dis	able
3. misspell	mis	spell
4. mislead	mis	lead
5. disband	dis	band
6. misshape	mis	shape
7. disclose	dis	close
8. dislike	dis	like
9. misfire	mis	fire
10. misinform	mis	inform

In the column at the right is a list of words with the prefixes "dis" and "mis." Match these words with the phrases on the left that could be used in place of the prefix words.

	Phrase	Prefix Word
j	1. to inform wrongly	a. distrust
e	2. to not band together	b. disable
d	3. to lead badly	c. misspell
h	4. the opposite of like	d. mislead
g	5. the opposite of close	e. disband
f	6. to shape wrongly	f. misshape
b	7. the opposite of able	g. disclose
i	8. to fire wrongly	h. dislike
a	9. to not trust	i. misfire
c	10. to spell wrongly	j. misinform

© Mark Twain Media, Inc., Publishers 98

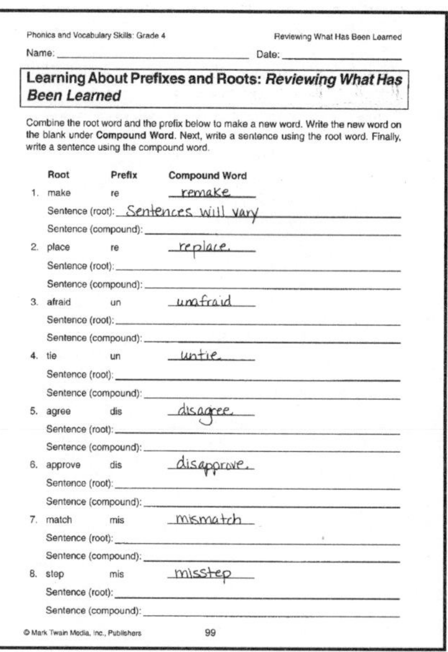
Phonics and Vocabulary Skills: Grade 4 Reviewing What Has Been Learned

Name: Date:

Learning About Prefixes and Roots: *Reviewing What Has Been Learned*

Combine the root word and the prefix below to make a new word. Write the new word on the blank under **Compound Word**. Next, write a sentence using the root word. Finally, write a sentence using the compound word.

Root	Prefix	Compound Word
1. make	re	remake
2. place	re	replace
3. afraid	un	unafraid
4. tie	un	untie
5. agree	dis	disagree
6. approve	dis	disapprove
7. match	mis	mismatch
8. step	mis	misstep

Sentence (root): Sentences will vary

Sentence (compound):

© Mark Twain Media, Inc., Publishers 99

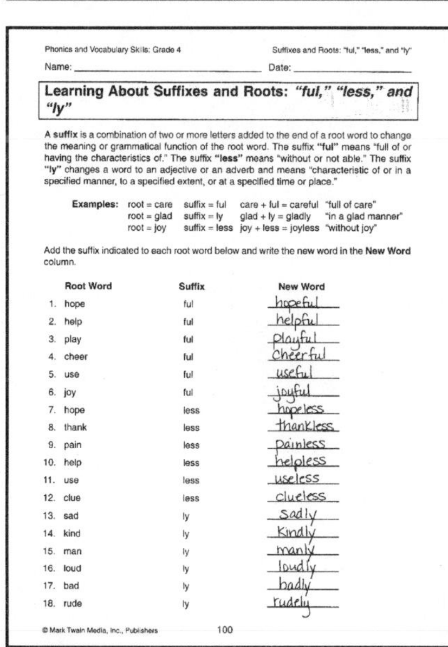
Phonics and Vocabulary Skills: Grade 4 Suffixes and Roots: "ful," "less," and "ly"

Name: Date:

Learning About Suffixes and Roots: "ful," "less," and "ly"

A **suffix** is a combination of two or more letters added to the end of a root word to change the meaning or grammatical function of the root word. The suffix **"ful"** means "full of or having the characteristics of." The suffix **"less"** means "without or not able." The suffix **"ly"** changes a word to an adjective or an adverb and means "characteristic of or in a specified manner, to a specified extent, or at a specified time or place."

Examples: root = care suffix = ful care + ful = careful "full of care"
root = glad suffix = ly glad + ly = gladly "in a glad manner"
root = joy suffix = less joy + less = joyless "without joy"

Add the suffix indicated to each root word below and write the new word in the **New Word** column.

Root Word	Suffix	New Word
1. hope	ful	hopeful
2. help	ful	helpful
3. play	ful	playful
4. cheer	ful	cheerful
5. use	ful	useful
6. joy	ful	joyful
7. hope	less	hopeless
8. thank	less	thankless
9. pain	less	painless
10. help	less	helpless
11. use	less	useless
12. clue	less	clueless
13. sad	ly	sadly
14. kind	ly	kindly
15. man	ly	manly
16. loud	ly	loudly
17. bad	ly	badly
18. rude	ly	rudely

© Mark Twain Media, Inc., Publishers 100

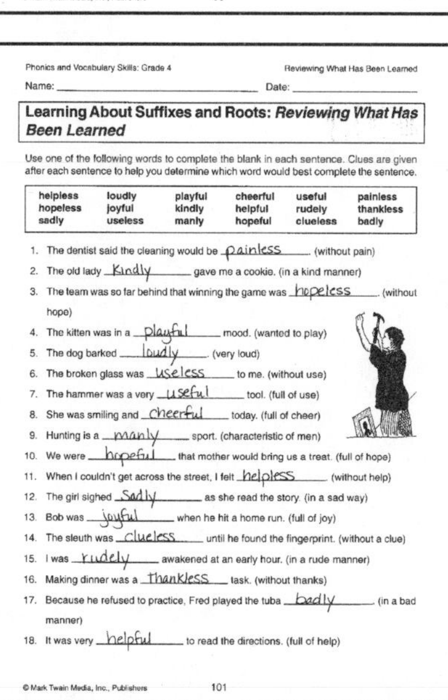
Phonics and Vocabulary Skills: Grade 4 Reviewing What Has Been Learned

Name: Date:

Learning About Suffixes and Roots: *Reviewing What Has Been Learned*

Use one of the following words to complete the blank in each sentence. Clues are given after each sentence to help you determine which word would best complete the sentence.

helpless	loudly	playful	cheerful	useful	painless
hopeless	joyful	kindly	helpful	rudely	thankless
sadly	useless	manly	hopeful	clueless	badly

1. The dentist said the cleaning would be painless (without pain)
2. The old lady kindly gave me a cookie. (in a kind manner)
3. The team was so far behind that winning the game was hopeless (without hope)
4. The kitten was in a playful mood. (wanted to play)
5. The dog barked loudly (very loud)
6. The broken glass was useless to me. (without use)
7. The hammer was a very useful tool. (full of use)
8. She was smiling and cheerful today. (full of cheer)
9. Hunting is a manly sport. (characteristic of men)
10. We were hopeful that mother would bring us a treat. (full of hope)
11. When I couldn't get across the street, I felt helpless (without help)
12. The girl sighed sadly as she read the story. (in a sad way)
13. Bob was joyful when he hit a home run. (full of joy)
14. The sleuth was clueless until he found the fingerprint. (without a clue)
15. I was rudely awakened at an early hour. (in a rude manner)
16. Making dinner was a thankless task. (without thanks)
17. Because he refused to practice, Fred played the tuba badly (in a bad manner)
18. It was very helpful to read the directions. (full of help)

© Mark Twain Media, Inc., Publishers 101

Phonics and Vocabulary Skills: Grade 4 One-Syllable Words

Name: Date:

Learning About Syllables: *One-Syllable Words*

The number of syllables in a word is determined by the number of vowel sounds heard when a word is pronounced. However, many words have vowel letters that are not heard. If a vowel is not pronounced, it does not make a syllable.

Write the number of vowels seen in each word in the **Vowels Seen** column. Write the number of vowels heard in the **Vowels Heard** column. Then write the vowel sound heard in the **Vowel Sound** column. Each word has **one** syllable. The first one has been completed for you.

	Vowels Seen	Vowels Heard	Vowel Sound
1. rain	2	1	long a
2. cage	2	1	long a
3. seen	2	1	long e
4. pain	2	1	long a
5. field	2	1	long e
6. team	2	1	long e
7. take	2	1	long a
8. seat	2	1	long e
9. pie	2	1	long i
10. lake	2	1	long a

11. In all of the above one-syllable words (a) two vowels are seen, but only (b) one vowel is heard when the word is pronounced.

Rule: The number of syllables in a word is determined by the number of vowel sounds heard, not the number of vowels seen.

© Mark Twain Media, Inc., Publishers 102

Phonics and Vocabulary Skills: Grade 4 Two-Syllable Words With the Vowel-Consonant-Vowel Pattern

Name: Date:

Learning About Syllables: *Two-Syllable Words With the Vowel-Consonant-Vowel Pattern*

Many words have two syllables. When a two-syllable word is pronounced, two vowel sounds are heard.

Example: begin

When a word has a consonant between two vowels (vcv pattern), the word is usually divided after the first vowel. Usually the vowel in the first syllable is long. The vowel in the second syllable is short.

Example: be/gin

Divide each of the following words after the first vowel. Write each syllable on the blanks provided. Read the sentence that follows.

Word	First Syllable	Vowel (long/short)	Second Syllable	Vowel (long/short/r-controlled)
1. begin	be	long	gin	short
2. pilot	pi	long	lot	short
3. tiger	ti	long	ger	r-controlled
4. soda	so	long	da	short
5. rodent	ro	long	dent	short
6. paper	pa	long	per	r-controlled
7. delay	de	long	lay	long
8. music	mu	long	sic	short

1. I will **begin** today.
2. The **pilot** flew the plane.
3. We went to the zoo and saw a **tiger**.
4. I will drink a **soda**.
5. The rat is a **rodent**.
6. Did you bring a pencil and **paper**?
7. The rain will **delay** the game.
8. The **music** was playing on the radio.

© Mark Twain Media, Inc., Publishers 103

Phonics and Vocabulary Skills: Grade 4 Two-Syllable Words With the Vowel-Consonant-Vowel Pattern

Name: Date:

Learning About Syllables: *Two-Syllable Words With the Vowel-Consonant-Vowel Pattern*

Some words with the vowel-consonant-vowel (vcv) pattern do not divide into syllables after the first vowel. The word is divided between the consonant and the second vowel. In words like this, the vowel sound of the first syllable is usually the short sound.

Example: The word **robin** has a vcv pattern. However, the word is divided between the "b" and the "i." rob/in

Divide each of the following words into two syllables and complete the blanks. Read the sentence following each word.

Word	First Syllable	Vowel (long/short)	Second Syllable	Vowel (long/short/r-controlled)
1. robin	rob	short	in	short
2. money	mon	short	ey	long
3. novel	nov	short	el	short
4. rapid	rap	short	id	short
5. linen	lin	short	en	short
6. river	riv	short	er	r-controlled
7. travel	trav	short	el	short
8. solid	sol	short	id	short
9. honey	hon	short	ey	long
10. liver	liv	short	er	r-controlled

1. The bird is a **robin**.
2. How much **money** does it cost?
3. I read the **novel**.
4. The car was moving at a **rapid** rate.
5. The tablecloth was made of **linen**.
6. We had a picnic by the **river**.
7. They plan to **travel** this summer.
8. The ice is frozen **solid**.
9. **Honey** is made by bees.
10. The **liver** is a large organ in the body.

© Mark Twain Media, Inc., Publishers 104

Phonics and Vocabulary Skills: Grade 4 Reviewing Two-Syllable Words

Name: Date:

Learning About Syllables: *Reviewing Two-Syllable Words*

Each of the following words has two syllables. Read each sentence to see how the word is used in the sentence. Divide each word into two syllables. Complete the blanks for each word.

Word	First Syllable	Vowel (long/short)	Second Syllable	Vowel (long/short/r-controlled)
1. comet	com	short	et	short
2. tulip	tu	long	lip	short
3. final	fi	long	nal	short
4. shiver	shiv	short	er	r-controlled
5. cupid	cu	long	pid	short
6. eager	ea	long	ger	r-controlled
7. cement	ce	long	ment	short
8. spider	spi	long	der	r-controlled
9. visit	vis	short	it	short
10. metal	met	short	al	short
11. gavel	gav	short	el	short
12. major	ma	long	jor	r-controlled

1. We saw the **comet** in the night sky.
2. That **tulip** is a pretty flower.
3. This is your **final** chance.
4. The cold air made me **shiver**.
5. **Cupid** was on the valentine.
6. She was **eager** for the game to begin.
7. We wrote our names in the **cement**.
8. The **spider** built a web.
9. I plan to **visit** my friend next week.
10. Gold is a soft **metal**.
11. The judge used her **gavel** to call for order.
12. The storm caused a **major** delay.

© Mark Twain Media, Inc., Publishers 105

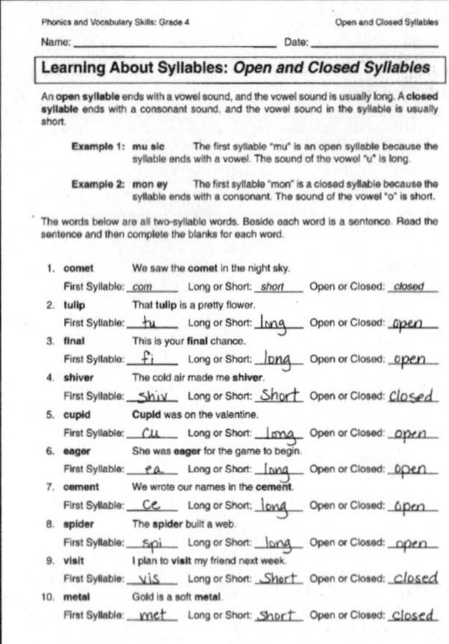

Phonics and Vocabulary Skills: Grade 4 Open and Closed Syllables

Name: ______________ Date: ______________

Learning About Syllables: *Open and Closed Syllables*

An **open syllable** ends with a vowel sound, and the vowel sound is usually long. A **closed syllable** ends with a consonant sound, and the vowel sound in the syllable is usually short.

Example 1: mu sic The first syllable "mu" is an open syllable because the syllable ends with a vowel. The sound of the vowel "u" is long.

Example 2: mon ey The first syllable "mon" is a closed syllable because the syllable ends with a consonant. The sound of the vowel "o" is short.

The words below are all two-syllable words. Beside each word is a sentence. Read the sentence and then complete the blanks for each word.

1. **comet** We saw the **comet** in the night sky.
   First Syllable: *com* Long or Short: *short* Open or Closed: *closed*
2. **tulip** That **tulip** is a pretty flower.
   First Syllable: tu Long or Short: long Open or Closed: open
3. **final** This is your **final** chance.
   First Syllable: fi Long or Short: long Open or Closed: open
4. **shiver** The cold air made me **shiver**.
   First Syllable: shiv Long or Short: Short Open or Closed: Closed
5. **cupid** **Cupid** was on the valentine.
   First Syllable: cu Long or Short: long Open or Closed: open
6. **eager** She was **eager** for the game to begin.
   First Syllable: ea Long or Short: long Open or Closed: open
7. **cement** We wrote our names in the **cement**.
   First Syllable: ce Long or Short: long Open or Closed: open
8. **spider** The **spider** built a web.
   First Syllable: spi Long or Short: long Open or Closed: open
9. **visit** I plan to **visit** my friend next week.
   First Syllable: vis Long or Short: Short Open or Closed: closed
10. **metal** Gold is a soft **metal**.
    First Syllable: met Long or Short: short Open or Closed: closed

© Mark Twain Media, Inc., Publishers 106

Phonics and Vocabulary Skills: Grade 4 Words That End With a Consonant + "le"

Name: ______________ Date: ______________

Learning About Syllables: *Words That End With a Consonant + "le"*

Many words end with a consonant plus the letters "le." Examples include tit**le**, ea**gle**, and no**ble**. The final consonant plus the "le" is a separate syllable.

Each of the words below is a two-syllable word ending in a consonant + "le." Complete the blanks for each word. Write a sentence using each word.

Word	First Syllable	Vowel Sound (long/short)	Second Syllable
1. title	ti	long	tle
Sentence: will vary			
2. eagle	ea	long	gle
Sentence:			
3. noble	no	long	ble
Sentence:			
4. rattle	rat	Short	tle
Sentence:			
5. little	lit	short	tle
Sentence:			
6. fable	fa	long	ble
Sentence:			
7. bridle	bri	long	dle
Sentence:			
8. maple	ma	long	ple
Sentence:			
9. middle	mid	short	dle
Sentence:			
10. bubble	bub	short	ble
Sentence:			

© Mark Twain Media, Inc., Publishers 107

Phonics and Vocabulary Skills: Grade 4 Open and Closed Syllables With the Consonant + "le" Pattern

Name: ______________ Date: ______________

Learning About Syllables: *Open and Closed Syllables With the Consonant + "le" Pattern*

In each of the following words, the **consonant + "le"** is a separate syllable. Complete the blanks for each word. Then write a sentence using each word.

Word	First Syllable	(Open/Closed)	Vowel Sound (long/short)	Second Syllable
1. cable	ca	open	long	ble
Sentence: will vary				
2. beagle	bea	open	long	gle
Sentence:				
3. bundle	bun	closed	short	dle
Sentence:				
4. bugle	bu	open	long	gle
Sentence:				
5. candle	can	Closed	Short	dle
Sentence:				
6. dimple	dim	closed	short	ple
Sentence:				
7. huddle	hud	closed	short	dle
Sentence:				
8. idle	i	open	long	dle
Sentence:				
9. boggle	bog	closed	short	gle
Sentence:				
10. spindle	spin	closed	Short	dle
Sentence:				

© Mark Twain Media, Inc., Publishers 108